PRAISE FOR

"If only I had had Marc's insight into my personal busyness earlier in my life, I would have been able to save thousands of heartbeats to spend with my grandchildren. The quiet perspective of *Less* will change how one works and how one lives."

— Warren Langley, former president of the Pacific Stock Exchange and managing member of GuruWizard Fund, LLC

"Like all great ideas, *Less* is disarmingly simple: know who you are, what you want to accomplish and why, and just do it, with a minimum of fuss and a maximum of joy. With gentle wisdom and real-world common sense, Marc Lesser effortlessly integrates profound spiritual wisdom into a clear and doable program for sane self-improvement, whatever the challenges of your work or life."

— Norman Fischer, poet, Zen abbot and teacher, and author of *Sailing Home: Using the Wisdom of Homer's Odyssey to Navigate Life's Perils and Pitfalls*

"An author who offers a book titled *Less: Accomplishing More by Doing Less* either really knows what he's talking about or is perpetrating a commercial fraud. Marc Lesser knows, and this valuable work is so loaded with practical, applicable insights and suggestions to simplify work and daily existence that after reading it I felt that I should be studying at Marc's feet. Marc and I have practiced Zen Buddhism in the same community for over thirty years. Yet I was surprised on page after page by how much I learned (and needed to learn) from my calm and unassuming friend. Give your daily life and work a spring cleaning by following the practices and path suggested in this book."

— Peter Coyote, actor and writer

"Marc Lesser dives into one of the most pervasive and persistent difficulties of our time — overwhelming busyness — with courage, deep practical know-how, profound spiritual understanding, and kindness. Any reader will be able to take up the methods he proposes to great and immediate effect — reducing stress and improving productivity with what really matters. You'll feel met and understood as you read and yet challenged to examine your actions, habits, and beliefs. Insights will abound, but the real payoff is taking them into your everyday life, and Marc shows dozens of ways to do that. *Less* goes way beyond most self-help books — yet stays within everyone's reach. Quite amazing."

— James Flaherty, founder of New Ventures West Integral Coaching and author of *Coaching: Evoking Excellence in Others*

LESS

OTHER BOOKS BY MARC LESSER

Z.B.A. — Zen of Business Administration:
How Zen Practice Can Transform Your Work and Your Life

LESS

Accomplishing More
by Doing Less

MARC LESSER

New World Library
Novato, California

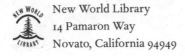
New World Library
14 Pamaron Way
Novato, California 94949

Text design by Tona Pearce Myers

Library of Congress Cataloging-in-Publication Data
Lesser, Marc.
Less : accomplishing more by doing less / Marc Lesser.
    p.   cm.
Includes index.
ISBN 978-1-57731-617-6 (pbk. : alk. paper)
 1. Contemplation. 2. Rest. 3. Time management. I. Title.
BV5091.C7L46 2009
650.1—dc22   2008044951

First printing, February 2009
ISBN 978-1-57731-617-6
Printed in Canada on 100% postconsumer-waste recycled paper

 New World Library is a proud member of the Green Press Initiative.

10   9   8   7   6   5   4   3   2   1

For Lee, Jason, and Carol
You bring hope, beyond words

You must learn one thing.
The world was made to be free in.

— David Whyte

CONTENTS

PROLOGUE: Accomplish More xiii

PART I
THE OVERWHELMING BUSYNESS OF OUR LIVES

CHAPTER 1: The Immense Sea 3

CHAPTER 2: The Art of Less 13

PART II
TRANSFORMING BUSYNESS
INTO COMPOSURE AND RESULTS

CHAPTER 3: The Less Manifesto 29

CHAPTER 4: Fear 37

CHAPTER 5: Assumptions 65

CHAPTER 6: Distractions 89

CHAPTER 7: Resistance 113

CHAPTER 8: Busyness, or Finding
the One Who Is Not Busy 133

Epilogue 155

Acknowledgments 161

Sources and Recommended Reading 163

Index 165

About the Author 173

ACCOMPLISH MORE

Having lost sight of our goals, we redouble our efforts.

— Mark Twain

THERE IS AN OLD STORY of a man riding very fast on a horse. As he rides past his friend standing on the side of the road, the friend yells, "Where are you going?" The rider turns toward his friend and yells, "I don't know! Ask the horse!"

The pace and intensity of our lives, both at work and at home, leave many of us feeling like that person riding a frantically galloping horse. Our daily incessant busyness — too much to do and not enough time; the pressure to produce a to-do list and tick off items by each day's end — seems to decide the direction and quality of our existence for us. But if we approach our days in a different way, we can consciously change this out-of-control pattern. It requires only the courage to do less. This may sound easy, but doing less can actually be very hard. Too often we mistakenly believe that doing less makes us lazy and results in a lack of productivity. Instead, doing less helps us savor what we *do* accomplish. We learn to do less of what is extraneous and engage in fewer self-defeating behaviors, so we craft a productive life that we truly feel good about.

Just doing less for its own sake can be simple, startling, and transformative. Imagine having a real and unhurried conversation in the midst of an unrelenting workday with someone you care about. Imagine completing one discrete task at a time and feeling calm and happy about it. In this book, I offer a new approach — what I call a "Less" Manifesto (and, by the way, that my name is Lesser is strictly a coincidence!) — that follows a five-step practice. I focus mostly on our work life, but the approach is equally useful for our personal life. In fact, the two hemispheres of our work and personal lives constantly reflect on and affect each other, each changing and/or reinforcing the other. And while the program requires some explaining on my part and patience on yours, I promise it is simple and enjoyable to follow.

Every life has great meaning, but the meaning of our own can often be obscured by the fog of constant activity and plain bad habits. Recognize and change these, and we can again savor deeply the ways we contribute to the workplace, enjoy the sweetness of our lives, and share openly and generously with the ones we love. Less busyness leads to appreciating the sacredness of life. Doing less leads to more love, more effectiveness and internal calmness, and a greater ability to accomplish more of what matters most — to us, and by extension to others and the world.

PART Ⅰ

THE OVERWHELMING BUSYNESS OF OUR LIVES

CHAPTER 1

THE IMMENSE SEA

If you want to build a ship, don't herd people together to collect wood and don't assign them tasks and work, but rather teach them to long for the endless immensity of the sea.

— Antoine de Saint-Exupéry

THIS BOOK IS ABOUT THE BENEFITS OF DOING LESS in a world that has increasingly embraced a crazy kind of more — more activity, more things, and even, strangely, more exhaustion. More running in circles to fulfill someone else's requirements. This book presents a different, calmer, and surprisingly productive way of approaching our work and life. But there are reasons we often drown in, or hide behind, long, jam-packed days. Why, in fact, *are* we so busy?

BUSY CAN FEEL GREAT

Of course, sometimes being busy can feel great. When we are busy earning a living, effectively leading others, achieving academically or artistically, and doing all the things that win us the admiration of partners, parents, and friends, we feel productive, satisfied, and emotionally and intellectually engaged in the business of life. This kind of busy energizes us; the other kind of busy leaves us bored, overwhelmed, and filled with a sense of failure. This book is about *that* kind of busy — that crazy, nonstop, way-too-busy ceaseless activity that exhausts our efforts and yet leaves us feeling as if we are getting nowhere. This is what I call busyness.

Frequent signs of busyness are debilitating stress, pretending and posturing to mask self-doubt, yelling or loss of emotional control, and avoidance of difficulties. This last point is particularly significant. Many of us inhabit a busyness-as-religion world where it is all too easy to fill our days with overwork or sensory overstimulation so that we don't have to face the difficulties or hard truths of our lives. If we are unhappy, busyness makes a convenient excuse so that we don't have to acknowledge what's not working in our jobs or our families. Sometimes stating how *busy* we are becomes code for "I must be (please, I hope I am) measuring up to expectations, because, after all, I'm constantly doing, giving, striving, achieving, and working just as hard as I possibly can!"

If we are unhappy, busyness makes a convenient excuse so that we don't have to acknowledge what's not working in our jobs or our families.

Then again, it's true that there *is* so much to do. People must eat. Humans get sick and require care. We have jobs to accomplish, businesses to run, things to fix. In any one day, there are all sorts of tasks — from the mundane to the certifiably daunting — that we would like to complete. Plus, beyond our personal welfare, many of us worry about the financial, environmental, and resource challenges facing our communities, our nation, and our planet;

these issues are enormous and, arguably, unprecedented. Our sense that there is too much to do is real and deserves acknowledgment and at times quite a bit of respect. Still, even in the face of daunting and overwhelming challenges, I have come to believe in the power of less.

DISCOVERING THE POWER OF LESS

When I was twenty-one years old, I took a one-year leave of absence from Rutgers University. This was one of my first experiences of choosing to do less — I realized that I needed to stop, to step outside the prescribed path of going directly from high school to college to developing a professional career. I needed to get another perspective about my choices and my life. This one-year leave turned into nearly ten years as a resident of the San Francisco Zen Center.

One of my work assignments during that time was to be in charge of the draft horse farming project at Green Gulch Farm (part of the San Francisco Zen Center) in Muir Beach, California, about five miles outside of Mill Valley. One of my teachers was Harry Roberts, a Yurok Indian–trained shaman, naturalist, cowboy, and Irish curmudgeon, and one day he asked me, "Do you want to know the three most important tasks of a human being?" I didn't hesitate to answer yes. "There are three tasks that matter in this lifetime," Harry said.

"The first task, though not the most important task, is to quiet the busyness in your mind. The second is to find your song. And the third task is to sing your song."

Harry's three essential tasks are what I now consider the essential underpinnings for transforming busyness into composure *and* results.

Quiet the Busyness in Your Mind

Harry Roberts spoke simply and directly about the practice of mindfulness long before that word came into more popular use. Mindfulness is the practice of paying attention to our inner life and the world around us. It begins by noticing how busy our minds are, how easily and habitually our minds jump from thought to thought, often residing in the past or in the future — anywhere but right here, right now. Quieting the mind generally begins with taking the time to be still, to be quiet, and paying attention to the breath and body. It does not mean we stop thinking, but we reduce the noise and increase our focus and concentration.

This process is like applying WD-40 to our minds. Increasing our awareness and paying conscious attention to our inner and outer life loosens the somewhat hardened or rusted parts of our thinking. Often, without even noticing, we get a bit stuck in mental habits and assumptions that underlie and drive our thinking. Applying some attention can loosen these patterns. This can mean increasing our ability to either narrow or expand our focus — whichever is most effective and refreshing to our habitual ways of thinking. Quieting the busyness in our mind can open the door to experiencing the sacredness of life in general and our own wondrous life even in the midst of everyday activities. It is something we can practice at any time, in any moment when we want to let go of the activity-driven busyness that can make us feel so depleted.

Find Your Song

Finding your song describes your ability to access your deep power — which is your appreciation for being alive. This embraces both who you are and all that you have right now as well as the greater possibilities you imagine and envision for the future.

We can hear our song only when our minds are quiet, when we can reflect on what is truly engaging and important to us — what brings us the greatest sense of belonging and of accomplishment. Finding our song means discovering our fierce and tender heart, where we feel deeply connected to all that surrounds us. Though our jobs and professional careers are important, our song is much deeper and wider than our work. Our song includes our way of being in the world, our personal relationships, our daily routines, and how we create a sense of community.

Sing Your Song

Results matter. Accomplishment *is* important. Your observable, concrete actions do have weight. At the same time, I believe part of Harry Roberts's message is that your song is always available. You can choose to sing your song — that is, have a positive effect on the task at hand and feel personally productive — anytime and anyplace, in small or large ways. Where you live and work and with whom you work matter tremendously. How you express your deepest longings and intentions is vitally important to enlisting others in your vision and in taking steps toward implementing that vision. Singing your song is simply a rather poetic way of reminding you that no matter what your circumstances are, you can engage them effectively and with as much personal satisfaction as possible.

Part of my song — which I have come to realize almost thirty years after Harry Roberts first posed that question to me — is to help others find and sing theirs by teaching the art of doing less. To me that means helping people

- reduce what is extra and unnecessary in daily life to increase the positive power that resides inside every human being;

- work and live with greater focus, energy, and composure; and
- align business, leadership, and contemplative practices with what is most meaningful and healing.

My hope is that the more we learn to quiet the busyness in our mind, discover our own song, and transform ourselves by expressing it, we will accomplish more of what really matters — to ourselves and to the welfare of the world.

ADDICTED TO BUSYNESS

We all get overwhelmed with busyness at times. But if you find yourself frequently comfortable with or bragging about how overbusy you are, you may want to question whether you've become addicted to being busy. Have you convinced yourself that you thrive on busyness? Do you often feel a physical satisfaction and increase in energy from "multitasking" — from the thrill of jampacking a day with more than seems humanly possible, or from the drama of working under impossible deadlines and meeting them at any cost to health and family? At the end of a workday, do you stay buzzed, and/or does the stress of the workday remain in your bones? When you are not working, do you have difficulty focusing and calming down? Do you feel a sense of emptiness?

If the answer is yes to most of these questions, you might want to consider developing a more sustainable approach to work and activity in general. Your current and future health probably depends on it.

It is particularly ironic that people specifically working toward sustainability — those in health care and medicine, those working for environmental reform and social change, and many in the nonprofit sector — often get caught up in a culture of busyness that overwhelms their work and personal lives and is anything but sustainable. In this poignant situation, people essentially trade their personal welfare for the common good. However, while I completely respect the scope and immediacy of the needs being addressed — the problems and suffering in our communities and our world are enormous and need urgent attention — I've found that pursuing solutions in a frenetic, nearly desperate way often leads to undesired or counterproductive results.

Almost without our realizing it, busyness has become a badge of honor. In the short term, the self-satisfaction it brings can feel really good. But busyness is not a sustainable way of life. Even when we throw ourselves into busyness with the best of intentions, it can become a way of avoiding deeper issues of purpose and meaning in our life, and it can harm the depth and authenticity of our connections with others.

OUR NOISIER, BUSIER WORLD

Not that many years ago, when you left work, you left your work. Now, wherever you go, your work can go with you: via cell phones, email, text-messaging, and the Web. With the ability to communicate whenever and however we like, we do, but the information flow can feel like an overwhelming geyser and the distinction between work and home is increasingly blurred. We can work not only while driving but when we are with our family, walking down the street, or eating at a restaurant. Sometimes this seems like a necessity: emails flow at such a whitewater pace that we become afraid of what will await us in the morning if we don't answer messages immediately (and again later that night). At home it is very easy and tempting to check email and voice mail and stay connected with work 24/7, which then comes to be what our workplace expects of us — that we will be available day and night. But all this vigilance and constant communication means we often try to do *everything* all the time at the expense of doing just one thing at a time. We sacrifice having time to think and reflect, we sacrifice being fully engaged with the people we are with (whether coworkers, friends, or family), and we jeopardize our own sense of ease and replenishment.

Of course the computer, the Internet, and cell phones are unmistakable boons to business. Technology in the digital age has streamlined so much of the way we conduct transactions and has improved the speed and often the quality of our work communications. It's just that we can become almost unwittingly addicted to the constant input until we forget we have the power to turn the technology off. This constant "connection" can make us confuse busyness with effectiveness, data with understanding, and talking or typing with real communication and emotional connection with those we are "connecting" with. This endless typing, texting, and technological multitasking allows little time for the quietude that can bring some satisfaction and composure back into our lives.

Often just twenty minutes, or even twenty seconds, of "time out" — time, literally, off — where we return to our breath and body, can do wonders for our brains, nervous systems, hands, arms, and backs. Even better, twenty minutes of meditation or contemplative practice, which will be discussed at greater length in chapter 4, is an always-available gift to ourselves. It is a great way to calm our mental circuits when they get scrambled and are about to blow.

DO LESS, NOT DO NOTHING

During the years that I was working on the manuscript of this book, I would mention its working title *Do Less, Accomplish More* to people. The two words "do less" really grabbed people's attention, as if I were throwing a life raft to those being pulled by a strong current down a river they didn't want to be traveling. The hunger for doing less is palpable. I see so many people who feel overwhelmed and frustrated with their work and personal lives. The list of what stresses us is almost endless. There are too many choices and too many worries and too little sense of accomplishment and satisfaction.

When I mentioned the working title, the enticing, almost fairy-tale image that would arise for some people was having the ability to sit on the sofa, feet up, doing nothing — while presumably the house magically and effortlessly cleaned itself. In the work-related fantasy, people imagined sitting at their desk, relaxing, perhaps surfing the Internet, and sipping a great cup of coffee — while emails stopped arriving, phones stopped ringing, tasks were completed, and yet somehow careers and income kept blossoming.

> I hope that doing less will enable you to determine, each day, what your true productivity and contribution can be.

Unfortunately, sitting on the couch or sitting at your desk is just that: sitting. This is not the same as "sitting meditation," which we will discuss later. Sitting and doing nothing is certainly one way to "do less," but it accomplishes less, too — and it is laziness or wishful thinking to hope otherwise. By advocating that we do less, I am not endorsing doing nothing or saying we must sacrifice productivity in our life. In fact, I am endorsing that endless immensity of the sea that Antoine de Saint-Exupéry beautifully alludes to in this chapter's opening quotation. Too often we spend our time busily hammering away and yet lose track of what we are building and why — and end up wasting our best efforts.

I hope that doing less will enable you to determine, each day, what your true productivity and contribution can be. Only you can define precisely what that immense sea is for you. Only you can know that which you truly long for, and only you can know the hard realities of what your life, both personal and professional, requires. My hope is that this book will help you see those things more clearly, as well as provide you with specific tools and strategies to accomplish those goals.

CHAPTER 2

THE ART OF LESS

The self is not a fixed entity, but a dynamic process of relationships. ...People are equipped to experience the sacred, to have moments of elevated experience when they transcend boundaries and overflow with love.

— David Brooks, *New York Times*, May 13, 2008

WHAT DO I MEAN WHEN I SAY YOU CAN DO LESS and yet accomplish more? Less and more of what? In fact, the particular activities in both cases must be determined by the individual, and often they are dictated by and change with circumstances. Doing less is more of an art than a science. The Less Manifesto I present in this book describes a more effective way of approaching life and work, and with this, we can do less and accomplish more — with a great deal more satisfaction — in nearly any situation.

The guiding principle is that when we approach any task in the right spirit, we become more successful and efficient at it. When we engage in fewer self-defeating behaviors, when we feel less fear, when we become less distracted, we accomplish more of whatever we set our hearts to. Thus, by recasting our attitudes, we reap tangible, practical benefits: we then "do less" by jettisoning activities we think are urgent but aren't; we "do less" by streamlining our efforts and eliminating unnecessary or reflexive responses. But to achieve these external real-world benefits, we first have to turn inward and "do less" within ourselves.

I will address these in more detail later, but here are five important ways we will learn to *do less*:

1. We do less by taking the time to rest mentally and physically in between or outside of our usual activities, perhaps instituting a regular practice of meditation, retreats, breaks, and reflection.

2. We do less by pausing in the midst of activities: mindfulness practice (such as coming in touch with our breath in between reading or sending emails) and walking meditation are two examples.

3. We do less by identifying and reducing unnecessary activities. In this case, "unnecessary" means those things that are not in alignment with what we want to accomplish.

4. We do less by the very quality of our being. We must be completely present for what we are doing, without sacrificing or rushing what's in front of us in order to get to "more important" stuff later. No matter how mundane the activity, treat everything as important and take pleasure in it. At bottom, whatever we are doing right now is *what we are engaged in* and it deserves our full attention and appreciation.

5. We do less by integrating effort with a feeling of effortlessness. This sounds like a contradiction but it isn't. With practice, we all can find that sweet spot that combines engagement, creativity, and composure.

What it means to "accomplish more" is even harder to define. Accomplishments can be big or small, and one's sense of accomplishment often depends as much on what we expect of ourselves as on what we've actually done. It may mean starting a year-long project or completing one; it may mean building a museum or waxing the floors of that museum. It could be writing a paper, graduating from school, changing careers, maintaining healthy relationships, growing heirloom tomatoes (or savoring the taste of those tomatoes), washing the dishes, or helping heal the world. It may mean simply planning each day or each week so that you balance personal, family, and work life. A sense of accomplishment is deeply personal, and it tends to shift as we grow. In addition, achieving specific goals frequently depends on more than our individual efforts; circumstances can thwart us even when we've done our best.

However, I would propose that we always *accomplish more* when we approach each moment and task in an open, relaxed, and fully engaged manner — whether leading a meeting, answering emails, or taking our children to school. In this way, our sense of accomplishment depends more on the way we act (which we can control) than on the results (which may be out of our control). No matter the chaos of any particular day, this can become one of our most important and useful aspirations and measures of success.

That said, in the workplace in particular, I'm a huge proponent of developing a vision and setting detailed goals. Short-term and long-term priorities are useful, important tools (along with benchmarks and revenue-and-expense projections, and so on). Of course, as we try to realize our vision, we invariably must make adjustments. Sometimes the greatest accomplishment is having the courage and skill to make intelligent midcourse corrections.

To accomplish more by doing less involves a simple yet profound transformation: it's a different way of being in the world. You may, in fact, be no less busy, but you will be less scattered and distracted, and you will accomplish *more of what matters to you*: more of what aligns with your deepest purpose and intention; more of what brings you satisfaction and connection with others; more of what you believe really needs to get done. Doing less and accomplishing more is about aligning your actions with your values and your particular passions. And finally, by becoming more peaceful and at peace with yourself, you will spread that into the world, which will become that much more peaceful and sane as a result.

> To accomplish more by doing less involves a simple yet profound transformation: it's a different way of being in the world.

ZEN TEACHER, BUSINESS LEADER

As with most people, my brain whirls every day with activity and accomplishment issues. I am no stranger to them or to the frustrations they engender. I'd like to share a bit of my background so you can better understand my perspective and how I came to develop a firm belief in the power of doing less while also managing to accomplish more. My somewhat unusual resumé includes Zen priest as well as entrepreneur and CEO, and I've found that the key to success is to integrate and balance the sometimes divergent principles of these two worlds.

As I mentioned earlier, I was an incoming senior at Rutgers University when I took a one-year leave of absence. I left New Jersey and headed to northern California. One day on my way to work as an office manager in downtown San Francisco, I got off the #6 Masonic bus, walked into the San Francisco Zen Center, and decided that this was the place I needed to be next. It offered a disciplined physical practice of daily meditation and work, an ancient tradition that had been adapted to our modern world; a philosophy and value system of radical openness and acceptance; and a community of people who were bright and sincere. I listened to a quiet but clear voice inside that said this was a place worth spending the next ten years. Instead of graduating Rutgers with the class of 1974, I graduated in 1984.

During those ten years I sat meditation every day, spent five years living in the Tassajara Zen Mountain Center (a Zen monastery), and worked with a variety of Zen teachers. I also had the opportunity to learn a great deal about the world of work and came to admire it tremendously. At the San Francisco Zen Center, work was seen as an integral part of a daily spiritual practice, and people were usually given jobs based not on their skills or previous experience but on what work might help stretch and challenge them.

During my years at Zen Center I was a dishwasher, kitchen worker, head cook, bread baker, and draft horse farmer. I ran a resort reservation office, and during my tenth year I was director of Tassajara. It was in this role that I first experienced the power of integrating ancient wisdom traditions and practices with cutting-edge thinking in leadership and business strategy.

Then, after finally graduating from Rutgers, I cast about for an appropriate graduate school and entered the New York University MBA program. There, I spent two years learning about business on Wall Street with a focus on management and entrepreneurship.

One of my first jobs after earning my MBA was working for Conservatree Paper, a distributor of recycled paper. In 1989, a few years into this role, I founded Brush Dance, a successful, innovative greeting card– and calendar–publishing company. During my fifteen-year tenure as CEO, Brush Dance combined quotes by the Dalai Lama, Thich Nhat Hanh, Rumi, and others with exceptional artwork and calligraphy, and our customers included major national and international retailers, like Target, Barnes & Noble, and Bed Bath & Beyond. In the first five years we grew from an idea in my garage to a company with more than $1 million in annual revenues.

Being CEO of a rapidly growing company in a turbulent retail environment was terrific instruction for learning about the challenges of business and the rigors of leadership. At the same time, I kept up my daily Zen meditation practice, which includes sitting in meditation every morning for twenty to thirty minutes, as well as always trying to integrate the health and healing of Zen practice into my everyday work and life. I became a Zen teacher, and in 2003, I was ordained a Zen priest.

In 2004, I combined my business and Zen practices directly when I founded ZBA Associates, an executive coaching and leadership consulting company, and in 2005, I wrote my first book, *Z.B.A.: Zen of Business Administration — How Zen Practice Can Transform Your Work and Your Life*. ZBA Associates facilitates business retreats and leads workshops in creativity and innovation, and its client list includes major corporations, small businesses, CEOs, and nonprofit organizations. My work life is now entirely dedicated to the passion I have felt for more than twenty years for integrating Zen practice with business practice.

COMPOSURE IN THE CRUCIBLE

I am proud of my work successes and of my accomplishments outside of work. At the same time, I have been sorely tested in the crucible of business, and I have learned a tremendous amount from failure and difficulty. Growing a company in the midst of a changing business landscape is full of ups and downs. I have lain awake at night worrying about how to meet payroll the next day or how to raise capital during difficult times. I've made heart-wrenching decisions to terminate people's employment. I launched an Internet company that failed.

One of the most important things I've learned is that satisfactory and even extraordinary results are always within reach if we can access real composure in the midst of activity, right in the center of our busy and stressful life.

One important way to do this is to access — and simply listen to — the various voices that reside within each of us. The simple, flat "I" that we so casually and often habitually refer to when thinking about or speaking about ourselves is actually a much more interesting and nuanced collection of "voices." For example, in response to the ubiquitous question "How are you?" I sometimes think, "Well, which voice shall I respond from?" I could answer the question from the voice of great success, of continuing struggle, or of tremendous failure. I could speak from the voice of plans and desires, of busyness, or of composure and satisfaction. I could respond in the voice of a family member, a friend, a spiritual practitioner, or a work colleague. All of these roles, feelings, and voices exist inside me and are true, and each contributes to defining my state of mind in any moment. At the same time, none of these voices completely defines me.

Becoming familiar with our many voices (and recognizing the many voices of others) can increase the depth of our personal awareness and self-understanding. This gives us more choices in how to respond to a situation and increases our flexibility in how we picture ourselves. This suppleness, I believe, simply makes us happier. Underneath, or perhaps at the center of, these voices is a larger, softer, and more subtle voice that is clear and composed; it comes from a place where nothing is lacking and where there are many possibilities. This is composure within the realm of effectiveness and productivity.

Though I will explore some of these concepts in more and greater depth later, here are a few visual images or metaphors of effectiveness. These images can be used in the moment to remind us to focus, to let go of the chatter of small "voices," and to access the central voice of composure that directs us to the most effective choices. Utilizing one or more of these images can guide us to bring more mindfulness into our everyday lives.

- A lever or fulcrum uses less effort to produce more results. What "leverage" increases your power or effectiveness in a situation? Is it being present and focused, being a caring as well as a smart leader, being a respectful and enjoyable collaborator on a team? Being a more patient listener?

- A carpenter cuts wood with a sharp saw, not a dull one. With a sharp tool, the same amount of effort leads to much more being accomplished. (Hint: You are the saw!)

- Life, like metal, appears solid and fixed, but with enough heat both become soft and flexible. Where can you apply the heat of mindfulness so that it softens the harder edges and unnecessary striving in your life?

- Like a tennis player, breathe and lower your heart rate between points. Work in bursts, relaxing in between periods of intense activity.

- Like a baseball batter anticipating a ninety-mile-per-hour fastball, narrow your focus when things move fast, so that you are prepared to swing and hit the ball with precision. Use the power of your attention to slow down your world without slowing down.

- Imagine yourself as the Buddhist icon of wisdom: one hand grounded, touching the Earth, the other hand holding a sword, a sword that can cut through confusion and chaos.

Try using any of these images during your day. For example, just having the intention to respond like a skilled tennis pro, meeting each challenge completely as it arises and then pausing to refresh and stay clear and calm before the next challenge comes, can influence the quality of your efforts.

These images (or any others you think of) work much better than the kinds of complaints I often hear from friends and colleagues, "I'm about to have a horrendous day!" or "I'm no good at this!" Stressful thoughts can become self-fulfilling prophecies. Thoughts, and the words we use, can influence our experiences and become our reality.

Here is an example of what this looks like in real life.

STOPPING IN THE MATERIAL WORLD

It is noon and I'm walking alongside a senior engineer, whom I'll call Robert, at a major technology company. We're leaving the parking lot, heading toward a building at the company's headquarters. The sun is bright and the acacia trees are in full yellow bloom. In my left hand I have my notebook of coaching issues we will explore today: strategic planning, team leadership, and budgetary concerns for the next quarter. We will also talk about ways to increase Robert's long-term leadership effectiveness. In my right hand are two black meditation cushions. Robert is holding his large and energetic white Labrador, Molly, on a leash.

Robert slides his employee badge through a mechanism by the front entrance doorway, and the two of us, the meditation cushions, and the dog pass through the security clearance area. As we walk up the stairs to a second-floor meeting room, we receive curious and bemused looks — not because of the dog but because of the cushions. Pets are not out of the ordinary here, but business meetings do not usually begin with sitting meditation.

Robert shuts the door to the windowless room, and he and I now begin our weekly executive coaching session with twenty minutes of meditation. We sit on the black, cotton-covered cushions, breathe deeply, focus our attention on being present, and just open our minds and hearts. Even the dog somehow manages to sit quietly.

When I first suggested starting our coaching sessions by meditating, Robert reacted like most people do, with skepticism. He felt he didn't have twenty minutes to sit and meditate during his typically crazy-busy workday, and even if we did, he couldn't help thinking it would only be "wasting time." Besides, he initially felt self-conscious and slightly ridiculous doing this at work, since he knew the reaction of many colleagues would range from amusement to disapproval.

Now, Robert finds that taking twenty minutes to sit quietly in the middle of the day — even a massively busy day at this thriving company's headquarters — increases his focus, clarity, and overall productivity. It calms and refreshes him and provides the possibility of taking that composure back into the fray of his workday and personal life. These benefits, both tangible and intangible, far exceed any cost of so-called down time.

Plus, I instituted meditation in our coaching sessions for a specific reason. When we began working together, Robert felt he lacked the executive skills needed to manage a team (his training was as a software engineer), and this aspect of his new executive position was beginning to feel nightmarish. Also, in general he felt overwhelmed and nearly burnt out by the intensity and fractured feeling of his twelve- to fourteen-hour workdays. After several months of working together in a coaching relationship with an emphasis on less doing — that is, less frenetic doing — plus daily meditation, increased focus, and strategies for working more closely and effectively with his team, Robert achieved several beneficial results:

- The overall productivity of his team increased dramatically, with a 30 percent increase in successful, new products launched.

- He went from feeling discouraged, anxious, and strangely unengaged from his work to feeling a much higher level of engagement and enthusiasm. He received a promotion to senior engineer, and, most importantly, he now feels able to cope with the increased demands that come with this new position.

- The team grew in size by 25 percent, and Robert found himself much more comfortable managing coworkers and eager to take on additional projects.

Of course, this is not the end of the story. Robert's life and work are complex, and with each success, new problems and challenges arise. But Robert's experience exemplifies one of my favorite quotes by Zen teacher Shunryu Suzuki, which is that despite our wishes, comparisons, and complaints, in a profound way "we all have just the right amount of problems." The challenge, and the real opportunity, is to develop the flexibility and responsiveness to fully meet, engage, and appreciate these so-called problems.

MORE KINDNESS AND LOVE

The art of doing less isn't merely about becoming more productive employees or businesspeople. The true benefit of focusing on

and taking a break from busyness is that it brings more kindness
and love into our lives. With less busyness and unnecessary effort,
more kindness and love can rise to the surface, leading to more
effectiveness, energy, and focus.
When we feel depleted, love is
the best replenisher — which
includes the love we feel for ourselves, the love we freely give
to others, and the love that comes to us from the people we care
for and admire most.

With less busyness and unnecessary effort, more kindness and love can rise to the surface, leading to more effectiveness, energy, and focus.

It's worth pointing out that the opposite seems to be true as
well. In our increasingly busy and impatient world, people seem
to be less kind and patient with each other. Much of that seems to
stem from busyness itself and from the increasing attitude that
being polite and caring is just another form of wasting time.

When we do less and begin to unravel many of the motivations, worries, and strivings that make us run in circles — and
when we stop trying to second-guess everyone else's motivations, worries, and strivings — what we find at the very core of
ourself and of life, I believe, is kindness and love. Those two glo-
rious things are the most profound levers for accomplishing more,
and more of what really matters.

This is not a radical idea. And yet, what a radical idea! What
a radical way to live your life! It underpins the best of psychological, spiritual, and contemplative practice. It is the fundamental
teaching of all great mystics and is the experience most of us hold
deepest in our hearts. We glimpse this basic truth whenever we
touch birth or touch death and experience a complete acceptance
of the simplicity and sacredness of being human. The more you
quiet your mind and let go of striving — which is all too often
someone *else's* concept of striving imposed on you — the less you

have to "do" and, miraculously, the more love springs forth from you. I believe that this simple formula is central to being a functioning, happy, and truly contributing human being.

Still, doing less takes courage. Stopping, pausing, reflecting, and fully doing one thing can be much more difficult than reflexively reacting and distracting yourself from what is most essential, most heartfelt, and most needed in your life. So let's get started. It's time to introduce the Less Manifesto.

PART II

TRANSFORMING BUSYNESS
INTO COMPOSURE AND RESULTS

CHAPTER 3

THE LESS MANIFESTO

It is vain to do with more what can be done with less.

— William of Ockham, 1288–1348

DOING LESS IS A RADICALLY SIMPLE IDEA, though implementing what is simple is not always easy. Often we are unaware of how complicated, frustrating, and ineffective we make situations when they needn't be that way at all. The Less Manifesto focuses on engaging *less* in five self-defeating habits in order to experience *more* ease — more composure and better results — within ourselves and with others. This can translate into more productivity, and productivity of a less exhausting sort!

The five categories, or habits, build upon one another. I have compressed each of the categories into one word — one behavior or activity that we can do less of — but each represents a huge arena of human emotion and psychology that can require much explanation and nuance to understand and transform. They are

- fear
- assumptions
- distractions
- resistance
- busyness

Each of these arenas can be debilitating, leading us to do more and accomplish less. They are often related or intertwined, creating problematic patterns of self-defeating behavior that contribute to unhappiness and dissatisfaction. If we don't address and change these behaviors, it doesn't really matter how much or little we do; we will always find it hard to accomplish what we want in a way that's satisfying. Ironically, as Robert discovered in the last chapter, once you change your behaviors, you often find you can do much more than before — and are eager to do so. This may be the opposite result of the vacation fantasy many people presume a "less" manifesto will lead to, but it's an immensely gratifying one.

In the Less Manifesto that follows, I describe each of these five arenas and provide exercises and practical advice for how to turn these negative habits around. Before I do, however, I think the best way to begin is to show how this works in practice.

LESS, AT WORK

Several years ago I was asked to lead a ninety-minute session during the second day of a three-day retreat for an organization's board of directors. The board was composed of CEOs and executive directors from around the country, and the purpose of the retreat was to develop the organization's strategic plan for the next two years. As I was about to walk into the conference room, one of the board members took me aside and informed me that the retreat was not going well and that they had just fired the facilitator. People were frustrated and anxious. "We have made little progress toward formulating our strategic plan," he said. "Welcome, and good luck."

As I walked into the room the tension was palpable. Stress was obvious in everyone's furrowed brows and body language. I introduced myself to the seventeen board members seated around the table and suggested that we begin with a brief period of meditation. About a third of the board members seemed delighted and made straight for the front of the room and sat on the floor or in a chair. About a third of the members seemed reasonably willing to comply and began to sit comfortably. Nearly a full third sat in the back of the room, faces tight, with arms or legs crossed. You could say they were not having it.

I rang a small bell and we sat quietly together. I gave some basic meditation instruction: Sit in a way that is comfortable and with energy; sit up straight with your back slightly arched, without leaning backward; keep your eyes open, looking down, without focusing; pay attention to your body and breath. As thoughts and feelings arise, just note them and return to your body and to your breath. Let yourself be curious, like a child, noticing your breath as though being aware of it for the first time.

While we were all sitting I spoke for a few minutes about the practice of generosity, of being open and kind to yourself and others. I mentioned the importance of paying attention to fears because they are real, but that fearlessness was a form of practicing generosity.

After about fifteen minutes of sitting I rang the bell and separated the board members into four groups. Each person in the group would have five minutes to speak, without interruption and without being asked questions. I suggested that each person address three questions, though they might sound unrelated to the scope of the retreat: 1) What is my purpose for being here on this planet? 2) How am I doing in relation to this purpose? 3) What steps do I need to take to align my purpose and my actions?

My thinking was that the members of this group needed to step back from focusing on the organization's strategy and instead find a way to connect with fellow board members and be more vulnerable with one another. Becoming more vulnerable with one another in this safe context might allow them to better understand who their fellow board members really were and how their deepest personal goals dovetailed with the larger mission of this particular organization.

I suggested that the person speaking in each group not try to look good or impressive or smooth. I further suggested that the person speaking might be surprised by the words that came from his or her mouth. I asked that the people listening give full attention to the person speaking rather than rehearsing what they would say during their time.

As the groups began to meet I could see that people were taking the questions I posed seriously. Group members huddled closely together. I spent some time briefly visiting with each group, listening to a variety of people speaking. There was a lot of emotion expressed: a lot of laughter and even a few tears, respectful listening and impassioned exchanges.

After about thirty minutes I called everyone back into the conference room. The energy of the group was transformed. The group felt more relaxed and connected. I asked how the smaller groups were for people. The first person who spoke said, "We should have begun our retreat this way! This is what was missing. We tried to begin working without stopping, without opening our hearts, and without connecting with each other." These words came from the CEO of a large technology company, someone who by his own admission didn't usually talk this way.

I left shortly after this session and learned afterward that the last day and a half of the retreat were extremely successful. The board reached a good deal of clarity and agreement on the organization's strategic plan. Several board members sent me notes expressing how important they thought the meditation had been. Others mentioned that slowing down and reflecting, thereby getting the discussion to a deeper, more effective level, had not only transformed the meeting but positively impacted the way they thought about structuring future meetings.

Three days after the retreat one of the board members, the CEO of a venture capital firm in Washington, D.C., sent me an email: she said she'd felt concerned when she'd heard about my proposed quiet time and was both cautious and curious about meditation practice. She usually strongly resisted anything that smacked of being "New Age" or, as she put it, "woo woo." She concluded: "If what we did is woo woo, I want more of that!"

It can be difficult to accept that to accomplish what we want often requires doing less, not doing more — especially initially. In this case, that meant putting aside the retreat's planned agenda and courageously taking time to be reflective. To move forward, everyone needed to step back and engage deeper questions, both of the organization's mission and of what each person hoped to realize for himself or herself and for the retreat. Slowing down or stopping (such as with meditation or other practices) is a very important part of doing less, but only one part. The retreat got off to a terrible start because the group was so intent on immediately tackling the most obvious question — formulating a

> It can be difficult to accept that to accomplish what we want often requires doing less, not doing more.

strategic plan for the organization — but this wasn't necessarily
the most important question. In order to work together at all, they
needed to be more open to one another and establish their common
ground first. It took courage and commitment to do this in an
agenda-packed, fill-every-minute environment.

During the session I addressed the five core categories of the
Less Manifesto:

1. Fear

People often bring a variety of unspoken fears into meetings — fear
of failure, fear of conflict, or fear of not achieving personal or organizational goals. Fear of not seeming productive. Forging ahead
with activity so as to counteract any fear that the retreat might be
viewed as a failure or that participants were "wasting time" very
nearly caused the retreat to blow up. The participants then plowed
ahead without acknowledging that the stress level had become
toxic and that something needed to change in the group dynamic.

2. Assumptions

Individuals assumed a level of trust and connection that would
allow them to engage in healthy conflict and disagreement, and as
a group, they assumed that just by gathering they would find a connection and a shared vision and understanding. In so doing they
nearly botched the main reason they had convened: for connection,
debate, and eventual consensus.

3. Distractions

Counterintuitively, strategic planning — the stated purpose of
the retreat — initially became a distraction. Particularly once
the intense negative energy arose, all efforts at planning became

counterproductive. This group needed to stop first, clear away all other distracting agendas, and consciously, as individuals, connect with their purpose, open their hearts, and connect with one another. Only then could they efficiently create a strategic plan together. It sometimes runs counter to an organization's culture, but putting meditation or group reflection at the beginning of a retreat is almost always a great thing to do.

4. Resistance

Many people in the group were initially resistant to the suggestion to stop the strategic planning process and sit quietly. This was not how these businesspeople usually approached solving a problem, and instead of being open to the idea, they clung to the way they thought retreats, and agendas, should typically be structured. But whenever things aren't working, we need to stop grasping at the way we think life should be in order to be open to new possibilities and solutions. As resistance in the group waned, they found the success they had been seeking all along.

5. Busyness

Our ninety-minute session increased the group's ability to work together, to focus, and to achieve the desired result. After meditating and reflecting, they got back to work. But they were able to do so because they had put aside the stressful busyness of the first day so they could now get down to business effectively. The group accessed something deeper than the drive toward an outcome, which I call "Finding the One Who Is Not Busy." In other words, in the midst of activity, we can always find a calm and connected center. This phrase, by the way, is taken from a Zen teaching story from the seventh century, a time when Zen practice, and apparently busyness, was flourishing.

Sometimes what looks like slowing down may in fact get us faster to a far more effective outcome. It was through the process of retreating and returning to what mattered that the group accomplished its goal of creating consensus around a strategic plan. By having the courage to step back and become more trusting of one another, they were eventually able to achieve what they intended to. And because everyone bought in, the results stuck.

> **Sometimes what looks like slowing down may in fact get us faster to a far more effective outcome.**

CHAPTER 4

FEAR

A mind that has any form of fear cannot, obviously, have the quality of love, sympathy, tenderness. Fear is the destructive energy in man.

— J. Krishnamurti

FEAR CAN BE A USEFUL ALLY. It can focus us, keep us safe, even at times keep us alive. Fear of illness or injury can motivate us to stop smoking, to exercise, and to eat healthier food. In our communities, it can motivate us to make our air and water cleaner, our bridges and levees stronger, our workplaces safer.

Fear can also be an enormous hindrance. Fear can color our world so that a stick can appear as a dangerous snake or an offer of friendship can be perceived as an imposition or even an attack. We can fear not getting promoted or losing our jobs; fear what people think about us, or fear that people aren't thinking at all about us. We can fear the loss of a loved one, fear getting older, fear dying. The list of possible fears is almost endless, so it is not surprising that, sometimes without our being aware of it, our actions and decisions can become ruled by fear. Living with fear can become an accepted and habitual way of being, leading to thoughts and actions that create more fear in a difficult-to-stop chain reaction — in ourselves, in relationships, in businesses and organizations, and in the world.

When we are afraid, our first impulse is to tighten our bodies and shut down our minds. We become the opposite of receptive and playful, and this is an enormous hindrance to learning new skills in the workplace, to collaborating, and to making interpersonal connections. The impulse to tighten can become so deeply ingrained that we may not even be aware of the ways that we keep ourselves back, or of the subtle and not-so-subtle ways that we communicate our fears to others.

Buddhism speaks of five primary fears:

- Fear of losing our state of mind
- Fear of public speaking or humiliation
- Fear of losing one's reputation
- Fear of losing one's livelihood
- Fear of death

Reducing fear (and its physical manifestation, anxiety) and opening oneself to new possibilities — surprises, even — is the first step, I believe, toward a more lasting sense of accomplishment. Reducing fear can be the first action that frees us to achieve a goal (even when, in losing our fear, our goal becomes something very different than previously imagined).

To reduce fear, however, we must acknowledge and become aware of our fears. This may sound daunting, but during the past thirty-five years of practicing Zen, I've noticed that this process of increasing awareness of fear is strangely freeing. My hope for myself, and my sincere hope for you, is that each day brings experiences in which fears are acknowledged without self-flagellation, so that these fears can be set free. This can allow wholly new approaches or solutions to appear.

It is no accident that fear is the first section of the Less Manifesto. It is the primary thing we need less of. Fear is like the "gunk" or rust that clogs our minds and our bodies, the perfect and beautiful engines we were born with. In our current world of more-faster-better, it can be difficult to see and feel the pervasive influences of fear. Transforming fear is not a one-time thing, either; we must develop ongoing strategies and habits to continually lessen it.

TIME AND FEAR

Two monks are arguing as they observe a flag blowing in the wind.

One monk states: The flag is moving.

The other asserts: The wind is moving.

A Zen teacher responds: Neither the flag nor the wind is moving. Your mind is moving!

The above Zen teaching story illustrates the power and influence of perception. We may presume to understand the world, and regard our understanding as obvious, but we are really seeing our limited conception of the world. In particular, we can feel especially challenged (and susceptible to fear) when we are presented with two diametrically opposed ideas, both of which are true.

There are many everyday examples of being confronted with paradox, but one that causes pervasive fear in our lives, and yet one that most of us, most of the time, give little thought to is time.

That is, we are obsessed with time, but we give little thought to our conception of time. In fact, in response to the increasing pace of our lives and our frantic busyness at work, many theories have recently been put forth regarding the best way to manage time. Some say to forget about old-fashioned time-management techniques and instead manage productivity. Others say that the real secret of avoiding busyness while staying engaged is to manage energy. Still others say that the key to success and satisfaction is to have a clear purpose, clear values, and a clear internal compass to cut through distraction and busyness. In a Zen way, I'm tempted to say: not time management; not productivity management; not energy management; not purpose management. Instead, manage your state of mind. In truth, I believe that all these approaches contain important elements, that all deserve attention.

> In a Zen way, I'm tempted to say: not time management; not productivity management; not energy management; not purpose management. Instead, manage your state of mind.

If it seems as though there is never enough time to accomplish all that we intend to do in a day, perhaps it's all Benjamin Franklin's fault. In 1784 he famously declared "Time is money." His intention was to motivate people to work more and shun "idleness." He worried about the young country's potential to generate industry and be innovative and industrious. How the pendulum has swung!

Today, one of the more insidious anxieties of modern life is fearing a lack of time. But time is an abstract human concept. The natural world flows seamlessly, a succession of days and nights, moons and suns. The natural world changes, but there is only ever the current moment. Once people invented calendars and clocks, they could measure and divide this endless flow, and time became a thing that could be "spent," "lost," or "wasted," and having a "shortage" of time became a source of stress. Now, if we have a task in front of us, we often pay more attention to the zipping-away, fleeting clock time — the hour or half hour or ten minutes we've allotted for finishing the task — than to the task itself. If a task takes longer than expected, if we rush and make mistakes, anxiety sets in, our breathing becomes shallower, and our sense of enjoyment and accomplishment disappears. Frequently, the more we're distracted by trying to beat the clock, the longer tasks take to complete.

But no matter how well we manage our time, the underlying problem and fear regarding time remains. To transform our fear, we need to change the way we think about and experience time. We have to think of time as more than a ticking clock.

Relative and Absolute Time

Relative time is clock time and psychological time. While relative time is an artificial human construct, it is a compellingly useful one. We can only plan and prioritize in the realm of relative time. Past, present, and future are essential tools for understanding, visioning, and planning. Once we've decided what is most important or essential to accomplish, relative time allows us to measure the future (in hours, days, or years) so we can successfully achieve it. In practice, this means reflecting on the past (how long did things take before?), weighing options (how long will it take if I do it this way or that way?), and effectively planning each day so that our time is "spent" effectively, rather than "wasted" by our constantly reacting to distractions or focusing on lesser priorities.

Absolute time is the unmeasured, ongoing "now" moment of the natural world, and it is equally important. When we enter the realm of absolute time, we see and experience ourselves and the world beyond the human construct of relative time. In absolute time, there is no "time." Instead, we become fully aware of and focused on the present moment and the activity in front of us, without regard to past or future. Paradoxically, as we become completely aware and present in absolute time, we also lose an awareness of ourselves. This is what the great thirteenth-century Japanese Zen teacher Eihei Dogen referred to when he said, "To study Buddhism is to study yourself. To study yourself is to forget yourself. To forget yourself is to awaken with everyone and everything."

We study ourselves in order to become aware of our conditioning, which is the sum of our past experiences. To understand our conditioning is to understand how we project our past into the present and the future. For example, when I say the word *sky*, you form an image in your mind of the sky. You know what the sky looks like because you've seen it before. But your image of sky might be different from mine. More importantly, when you step outside, you might not pay any attention to the sky because you think you already know what it looks like. You've seen it countless times. However, in truth, the sky is new every moment and never the same — it is always changing, sometimes subtly, sometimes dramatically.

The same is true of ourselves. We think we know who we are, for we have been conditioned by our past experiences. As with relative time, for the sake of convenience, we become set or fixed in our ideas of ourselves — so that we unfold with a reassuring predictability, like the hours of a day. Within the realm of absolute time, however, these increments, these labels from the past, do not exist. Human constructs based in relative time disappear. Experiencing absolute time is to experience the world as it actually is in the moment, and doing so requires that we loosen our ideas and constructs.

When we drop our conditioning, it's quite remarkable how the ordinary becomes extraordinary: the sky comes alive, the flowers come alive, time comes alive, and our experience comes alive. In this state of aliveness, we are more composed, more ready, and more productive. This sense of aliveness instills a fresh sense of meaning in one's activities and relationships. It also opens up new possibilities, since we are no longer bound by our past. The result is increased focus, creativity, and productivity. And less fear.

In talks and in her book *My Stroke of Insight*, neuroscientist Jill Bolte Taylor describes in great detail the experience of seeing herself in the midst of having a stroke. During the stroke, she became poignantly aware of how the left side of her brain had stopped functioning. Because she only had use of the right side of her brain, time stood still and all rational, comparative thinking came to a standstill. As a result, she experienced great joy and bliss. She experienced a quality of serenity and openness that was completely new and compelling, providing new insights into meaning, love, and total acceptance. Then, realizing she was having a stroke and had to get help, she was able to gain some access to the left side of her brain in order to dial the telephone. Clearly, we need the left side of our brain, but Taylor's message is: Don't forget about the right side of the brain. Don't live a life that ignores the timeless and incomparable state of mind that is always available to us.

What's wonderful is that we don't need to choose between relative time and absolute time. As in the Zen teaching story about the flag, we can embrace all simultaneously — the flag, the wind, and our mind. Within relative time, we can plan and prioritize wisely — doing what matters most, first. But within and in between our doing, we can enter absolute time, where each moment is new, and where every activity we undertake feels (and is) fresh and alive.

Playing with Time

Here is a way to practice and play with time.

Each day, decide one thing that you want to accomplish. Create a written list of next steps and associated dates when each of these steps will be initiated and projected completion dates.

Each day, spend some time totally unconcerned with time. You can do this by bringing your attention to your breath and your body, for a period of three breaths. Or, bring your attention to flowers or trees or the sky, seeing them as if for the first time. For part of each day, let go of your to-do list.

WE ACCOMPLISH MORE IN A FLUID WORLD

Often when I walk into a company or organization as a coach or consultant, I am struck by the feeling that everyone working there is attempting to change an environment that they, in the sinking pit of their stomachs, believe is solid, immovable, and permanent. As a result, fear underlies almost every activity and communication. Fear of change, fear of failure, and fear of conflict are particularly common.

In the face of this sense of solidness, of dismaying immutability, I see people working harder — they work more hours, and with more intensity, but also with more frustration. Albert Einstein said, "Insanity is doing the same thing over and over again, and expecting different results." In order to lessen fear, and to change a toxic environment, we have to change how we perceive the situation and how we work. This is not easy, of course, especially when the predominant culture is rooted in fear and responds to it with frantic nonstop busyness.

Harry Roberts — the same person who spoke of "songs" — was my welding teacher at Zen Center's Green Gulch Farm, and he was the first person in my life to introduce me to this concept of accomplishing more by doing less as it relates to work. As a young Zen student, I was charged with the daunting task of farming by using horses instead of tractors, and I struggled to learn the vital skill of repairing old horse equipment.

Harry taught me that the secret to welding is to see and

understand that the natural state of metal is actually liquid. What we call metal is in fact liquid that has become solid. By applying heat to metal, we soften it, returning it to its original condition, and we can then shape the metal with very little effort. Attempting to shape metal when it is too cool and solid requires tremendous effort and doesn't accomplish very much.

As Harry shared this "secret" of welding with me, he let out a hearty laugh and said that this is also the secret to living fully as a human being: we as human beings, our world, and time all appear to be solid. Our perception of and belief in this solid world lead us to act in ways that are much like attempting to shape metal while it is still solid and completely hard. At the time this was a very radical thought to me, and I too laughed heartily.

Our minds and bodies are considerably more fluid than we assume; everything in our world is less permanent than we conveniently and conventionally imagine. This was an "aha" moment for me, a lasting gift from Harry Roberts, still one of the greatest teachers I have studied with. I have been digesting and applying this lesson for much of my life. That lesson is this: if the metal doesn't bend, don't hammer harder — apply more heat. Particularly concerning ourselves, our beliefs, and our relationships, everything is malleable. Once we understand and embody the fluid nature of our world, we reduce our fear and dramatically increase our ability to accomplish more with less effort.

Where do we find this heat? To use the terms above, by letting go of relative time and entering absolute time through focused attention and mindfulness practice. Much like the process of applying heat to metal, retreats, meditation, and mindfulness practices act to soften ideas, views, and emotions that have become hardened. Using them, we can stop reliving the past and thereby loosen the solid quality of our fear of what might be.

MEDITATION: THE RADICAL PRACTICE OF SITTING

Each of us has a mind with great potential. We have the possibility
of creating a world of compassion and well-being and we have
the capacity for mindless violence and destruction. A second
powerful lesson has been in the profound plasticity of the human
brain. We can actually focus our minds in a way that changes
the structure and function of the brain throughout our lives.

— Daniel J. Siegel

Meditation could be described as the simple and radical practice of
sitting. It's the practice of learning to see and receive what is
right in front of you and accepting it. Slowing down, sitting,
breathing deeply, and opening your awareness allows you to discover more textures, thoughts, feelings, and perceptions — and
this awareness can be brought back to the world to change your
experience of it. As Shunryu Suzuki, founder of the San Francisco
Zen Center and author of *Zen Mind, Beginner's Mind*, so aptly
stated, "The world is its own magic."

Not all of these new discoveries will be pleasant. In meditation, to see and accept everything includes one's own painful
emotions, impatience, and unmet aspirations. This is useful,
because these things typically feed our fears; they form the basis
of the assumptions and predictions that usually predominate in our
thinking. Meditation develops our ability to see the sources of our
emotions and thoughts — and to see these sources with more composure — making meditation an excellent way to understand and
transform fear. By practicing with curiosity, acceptance, and openness you can become more friendly and lighthearted in relationship to fear. This practice opens pathways to becoming more
honest with yourself, more self-accepting, and in the process
more compassionate toward others.

I have been meditating each day for thirty-five years, and it has helped me to accept the many voices and emotions within myself. Through it, I have also learned to (sometimes) access my quiet and calm center in the midst of noise and turbulence. I'm convinced that this calm center exists within everyone. For me, to sit quietly for thirty minutes each morning is much like the act of brushing my teeth. It's not so much about doing something special or extra; it's just that I would feel odd if I didn't spend time in this way each morning. It's basic maintenance, providing me with greater composure and clarity about the day's possibilities and inevitable disappointments than I would have if I did not sit quietly.

Meditation is a bridge between not doing and doing, a tool that we bring from one state to the other so that "doing" is improved by having access to our quiet, calm center. Through meditation, we have an opportunity to see and experience ourselves as more than all the various voices and emotions that we think of as our personality. We develop a place of quiet that we can access anytime.

The best way to create this is to follow a regular meditation practice, typically daily or several times per week. This is easiest to do if you set a consistent time for it, whether in the morning, in the late afternoon, or as the last activity before you go to sleep. While all meditation helps, regularly practicing self-awareness brings increased benefits to your work, emotional life, and relationships. More attention and scrutiny very often result in more harmony. With practice you become more skilled: you become more adept at aligning your life, more integrated, more effective, more productive, more creative, and more at ease.

As at the board of directors retreat I describe in the previous chapter, some people resist meditation, feeling that they have hundreds of more "important" and "urgent" things to do than to "just sit." Experiencing resistance isn't unusual, particularly when meditation promises to bring us face to face with our fears. Don't we think about those enough as it is?

But imagine: Wouldn't it be refreshing to take time at the beginning of each day to simply appreciate being alive — time with no expectations, time with absolutely nothing to accomplish, time outside of your judgments? Imagine just appreciating your breath and your body, being open to and aware of the magnificence and mystery of your human existence. Imagine just observing and being curious about the thoughts, problems, emotions, and complex stories that make up your "I." Isn't this an experience of the opposite of fear?

So, don't delay. Begin a meditation practice. Mark it on your calendar! Try sitting every morning for the next five days, then the next five days, then the next five years; you might want to ask a friend to join you. Find or create a meditation group. You don't need any fancy cushions or candles. Just sit, for twenty or thirty minutes. Even ten. Congratulations in advance on beginning or continuing this simple and profound practice of "just sitting."

Meditation Practice

Try this right now. Wherever you are, take a few deep breaths. With your eyes slightly open and looking down, bring your attention to your body. Notice any places (such as your shoulders, neck, back, legs, feet) where you may be holding or feeling tension. Try briefly tightening and relaxing these places.

Pay attention to your posture: sit up straight, with your stomach gently pushed out and shoulders back, and your back slightly arched. As you check in with your body, pay attention to your breath. Yes, you are breathing! Now breathe fully, letting your lungs fill completely; then breathe out, slowly and fully.

As you pay attention to your body and your breath, let your

awareness expand to the sounds around you. Notice the smells. As thoughts and concerns and worries arise, return your attention to your breath and body. Notice you are alive! Appreciate this. Just be aware of and curious about whatever arises. Continue observing your breath, your body, your thoughts, and yourself, with nothing else to do or accomplish. When you are done, take a few moments to gradually reorient to the rest of your day.

During meditation, as you begin to focus on your breath and your body, you may notice your heart beating more slowly, the very act of your breathing becoming a focus, and that your breathing happens without your having to do anything. Your breathing may deepen and lighten at the same time. If your mind speeds up and you find yourself flooded with thoughts, that's okay. If you feel more relaxed and notice that your mind more or less slows down, that's okay, too. Unlike with almost any other place in our lives, there is no right or wrong here, and this is perhaps the key. Meditation is stepping outside of our judging, comparing, evaluating world, and that is why it is so valuable and pleasurable. After all, we are human beings, not merely human doings.

I find it sometimes embarrassing being a meditation teacher — teaching people the radical practice of not doing! What could be simpler and more obvious? Just sitting; just being aware; just allowing and expressing your own human dignity, self-sufficiency, humility, and courage. A paradox of meditation practice is that the more you can give up wanting or expecting anything, the deeper your relaxation, healing, and ability to live more fully and effectively. The more relaxed, aware, and awake you become, the greater your ability to accomplish more with less effort.

> A paradox of meditation practice is that the more you can give up wanting or expecting anything, the deeper your relaxation, healing, and ability to live more fully and effectively.

Meditation can be seen as a grand yet simple experiment, with you as the laboratory. During your meditation practice, experiment by asking yourself these questions:

What am I feeling?
What's behind those feelings?
And what's behind those feelings?

Your answers, and the emotions that arise, may surprise you and challenge some of your most basic assumptions. You may notice:

- Your mind won't turn off. You may experience a surprising amount of noise and constant chatter in your thoughts. Just notice, appreciate, and welcome all that arises in your meditation practice.
- Your thoughts actually slow down and become still. At first, when you notice this, you will lose the moment, but simply return to your body and breath until the distractions ebb again.
- Your emotions, dreams, and aspirations may come powerfully to the surface. Pay attention. What is there for you to learn?
- You may find you are more than your thoughts; more than your fears, worries, and plans.

Counting Your Exhales Meditation

There are many varieties and styles of meditation. One experiment to try during your meditation is to count your exhales from one to three; then return to one. This practice provides structure and focus to meditation practice. While increasing your ability to focus on one thing, this practice highlights the fluid nature of your consciousness. You may find, as I sometimes do, that you count "one" and never make it to two — with the mind darting with lists, worries, and dreams. This practice can be humbling, and at the same time it can assist you in experiencing the fluid nature of your body, your mind, and the world.

Mindfulness Practice

Mindfulness involves simply giving yourself over to your senses (or perhaps better put — coming to your senses!). Right now, notice the weight of your body in your chair or on the floor; see the quality of the light in front of you; listen to the sounds around you; feel your feet on the floor or curled up under you; feel your hands holding this book. Notice the sensations in your body, notice your mood. Surrender to awareness, and to the awareness of the fluidity, the ever-changing quality of your breath, body, and thoughts.

In fact, the word *mindfulness* is a bit deceiving, since mindfulness is more like the practice of emptying — letting go of your preconceived ideas, getting "out of your head," and awakening your senses to what you see, hear, smell, taste, and touch.

To get a feel for the difference between mindfulness and not-mindfulness, notice right now what you are seeing, hearing, smelling, tasting, and touching. Now think of the year you were born and divide it by three. I imagine you found it easy to go from being mindful to thinking and calculating in your head, and it's sometimes just as easy to go in reverse. Mindfulness is available at any moment. Much of our work demands that we think, plan, and calculate — that we inhabit our minds — but there isn't an engineer, lawyer, doctor, or teacher who doesn't also need to be aware of others, to be emotionally open and able to communicate well. When we have to move quickly from spreadsheets to conferences, or if we just need a little more heat to soften stuck thoughts or emotions, mindfulness provides spaciousness and flexibility, helping us to keep from acting out of fear.

Journal Writing, or the Benefits of Talking

The practice of writing in a journal has numerous benefits. Much like meditation, it offers a chance to pause, stop, and reflect outside the world of activity. Writing in a journal over time, and then reviewing what we have written, provides a tool for seeing and understanding our thinking. We can follow the fluidity of our thoughts as well as how we think. Which emotional issues recur, and which don't? Do the issues and events that challenged us last week or last year continue to challenge us? How have they evolved, eased, or intensified? This process of writing, reflecting, and reviewing is another way we apply heat to our seemingly solid self — softening, opening, and allowing for choices in how to shape ourself and our world.

If journal writing doesn't appeal to you, try to find an equivalent, perhaps by talking: regularly — at night, in the morning, or sometime during the day — talk to your spouse or partner, a close friend, or a mentor about issues that are troubling you or that are particularly engaging your mind and your energy. Clarifying our thoughts through the exercise of regular conversation can be another great way to open ourselves to newer and deeper ways of thinking.

RETREAT TO REDUCE FEAR

If you think you don't have the time to take a yearly retreat, or fear that retreats are themselves a waste of time, I suggest you reconsider.

Each fall Bill Gates, founder and chairman of the board of

Microsoft, spends a week in reflection because he believes in the power of retreats to renew and refresh himself and his business outlook. According to *The Wall Street Journal*, during his seven-day "Think Week," he considers the future of technology and how Microsoft should respond. *Time* quoted Gates as saying, "We have retreats each year where we think about where the world is heading."

When Gandhi was at the height of his work and unexpectedly found himself receiving worldwide attention, someone asked him, "You are living in the midst of so many pressures. How have you managed to respond to all the expectations and still maintain your equanimity and grace?"

Gandhi responded, "I used to take a monthly retreat each year. Now I must take two months of retreat each year."

I generally take part in an annual six- to seven-day Zen retreat in the redwood forests of northern California. One of the main reasons I take part in retreats, and believe so powerfully in them, is that being on a retreat gives me time to address my deepest fears. While this method for engaging fear is still somewhat unusual in the West, many cultures around the world have used some version of a retreat for centuries to settle the mind and face our subtle and not-so-subtle fears.

At the typical Zen meditation retreat I attend, each day consists of a series of thirty-minute periods of meditation from 5 AM to 9 PM. These are interspersed with periods of walking meditation, silent meals, a work period, and some rest time. Other retreats operate differently — there is no average or typical retreat — but over the years, after having done many retreats, I've noticed that there is a consistent pattern to the experience. Here is what I've found.

Day one can be pleasant and restful. The contrast between the pace of my life and completely stopping and not having to do anything can be a relief. At the same time, beginning a retreat can be a shock to my system. Stopping and sitting allows me to become aware of the usual speed and intensity of my life. This awareness and the process of stepping outside of my usual activities can bring emotional pain and a sense of dismay as well as joy and relief.

During day two, some boredom and questioning arise, generally around issues of doubt: in particular, "Precisely why am I doing this?" Why would I want to spend my time sitting here, looking at nothing, when there are so many other things in my life that need attending to, some urgently? This is especially true when the weather is nice, or quite frankly, no matter what the weather is like. The emotional tone of these questions or doubts can range from quietly irritating to at times loud and painful.

On day three, the intensity of my questioning and complaining tends to increase. Then I mix in some distraction and some whining to myself. I also become more and more aware of the stories I tell myself, about my problems, fears, and aspirations. I usually begin to feel physical discomfort as well. Soreness in my legs and lower back usually increases my interest in doing anything other than being here, sitting.

By the middle of the fourth day, I usually reach a point where I become completely tired and bored with the same old complaints and stories: my same old tapes, my same old views of who I am and what I am doing and what I am not doing. This is what I call the "sick of myself" day. I become fed up traveling down the worn ruts and alleyways of my mind. These include my fears: fear of failure, fear of not being able to support my family, fear of being exposed as not very smart, and on and on. Mental discomfort and physical discomfort become difficult to distinguish. I spend so much effort trying to push away this discomfort that my

defenses begin to wear down. I start to give up and surrender to
a deep sense of knowing, as well as comfort in not knowing.

The final two or three days are much less predictable. Of
course, I still have lingering complaints; my inner dialogue
includes moments of questioning and being sick of myself. At
the same time, moments of true calm and quiet arise. I feel more
space, connectedness, and possibilities. I feel less constricted.
Specifically, many of my fears begin to ebb. Precisely because
I've spent so much time looking at them, they now feel a bit boring! My defenses and questioning become increasingly distant. As
these move into the background, I catch glimpses of something
beyond my being embedded in this time and this place, while
simultaneously feeling completely rooted in this time and place.
The ordinary and extraordinary, the mundane and sacred, begin
to merge. I experience much more humor and lightness. Sitting and
looking at a wall begins to feel outrageously funny, even quite
pleasant. Food during the meal breaks tastes better. Colors around
me look sharper. People appear miraculously beautiful and precious. I see deep joy and pain in the faces of others. My own face
probably projects a blend of ease, struggle, sorrow, and enjoyment
as well.

These stages are not particular to a Zen retreat but rather follow a common pattern of slowing down, resistance, struggle, recognizing patterns, putting aside the struggle, and finally acceptance
and transformation. A similar experience can be had on shorter
retreats, even of just a day or half day, but they are usually less
intense. We always benefit whenever we consciously step outside
of our regular routines and life. However, longer retreats are
most successful when they are structured, so you have support and
guidance to get you through the particularly challenging parts that
would, ordinarily, make you want to get up and do anything else.

The Path and Process of Retreat

Be thoughtful in the way you choose a place and a time for your retreat. If you have not taken retreats before, I suggest finding a group that offers one- to seven-day retreats. Do some research; ask friends for referrals. Check the Internet, and don't overlook calling the nearest Zen center, your place of worship, or the Wellness Center of a hospital for suggestions. Then when you've found a retreat that feels right, sign up, put it on your schedule, and protect the time.

Retreats come in many shapes and sizes. Here is a list of options to consider:

PERSONAL RETREAT: Create a retreat for yourself, or include a friend or small group. Make it one or two days, and create a schedule that gives the retreat a simple structure. Make sure to eliminate potential distractions, and give yourself several opportunities for focused silent meditation, whether sitting or walking.

MANAGEMENT RETREAT: Many of the most highly effective management teams I know take a one-day retreat each quarter and a three-day retreat each year. This time can be used to build trust, to clarify strategy, and to move toward a shared vision. Building trust takes time. Working with a skilled outside facilitator can help foster more open communication. The results, both in better relationships and improved performance, are well worth the time and effort.

STAFF RETREAT: Structure a retreat for your staff. Include everyone if you are part of a small company, or if it's a large company, take just your team or division. Here again, the goals are building trust, creating strategies, and strengthening your shared vision.

FAMILY RETREAT: It can be hard for families to slow down, stop, and take a retreat. Structure a way for your family to spend time together, without all of the toys and distractions of a typical vacation. Camping, river rafting, or any variety of outdoor activities can provide a supportive environment for stepping outside of your family's usual pace.

WEEKLY "SABBATH": There is tremendous wisdom in the ritual of taking one day off each week as a Sabbath or a day of mindfulness — a day of no work, no shopping, no watching TV, no using the computer. Try creating a regular, consistent day when you will not do anything that resembles commerce or engaging in your typical forms of entertainment and distraction.

When you go on or create your retreat, here are some things to keep in mind:

CHANGE THE PACE: Slow down. Structure a day, or part of a day, where the focus is on paying attention to yourself and your surroundings when you have nothing to accomplish. Slow down the pace from your usual activity level by removing all external distractions. Leave your cell phone and BlackBerry behind.

FIND A NEW PERSPECTIVE: If possible, retreat away from your office space and home space. Be in a place that is less familiar and where you are less apt to feel the pull of everyday tasks and usual routines. Quiet and spaciousness are very important.

GET TO KNOW YOUR MONKEY MIND: Don't be surprised or discouraged if you notice how busy and noisy your mind is at the beginning of your retreat. In Buddhist practice this is sometimes referred to as "monkey mind," the mind that is always jumping around from tree to tree. Just pay attention to it; stay with and be curious about monkey mind. Use your meditation and mindfulness practices; come back to your breath and body.

BECOME SICK OF YOURSELF: Pay attention to the patterns and habits of your thinking. Stay with the stories you tell yourself — what you could be doing instead of being on retreat, how bored and uncomfortable you are, what a waste of time this is, how frustrating it feels to repeatedly face your fears, and so on. Let yourself become sick of yourself.

FIND YOUR CENTER: Notice that you are more than your stories. In the busyness of life, you can easily become fooled into believing that the stories you tell about yourself are you, and that they absolutely define you. As your mind becomes more quiet, you gain access to your still, undefinable center. You glimpse the ways you create these stories about yourself, about others, and about the world. Are these stories necessarily true? What if the opposite is true? Could both versions of the story be true? Who is it that is creating these thoughts? Find your center beyond your stories, beyond your personality. This is the realm of all that you are and have the potential to be.

> In the busyness of life, you can easily become fooled into believing that the stories you tell about yourself are you, and that they absolutely define you.

REFRESH AND RENEW: Allow yourself to step (or more accurately, drop) into a place of not knowing, of uncertainty, of joy and refreshment. See if you can just

appreciate everything you are, even your doubts and discomfort; just appreciate being alive.

BLEND THE MUNDANE AND THE SACRED: See and appreciate the gamut of life — from the immensity and sacredness
of all existence to our need to earn a living and even to our
need to eat and afterward wash the dishes, sweep the
floors, and clean the counters.

LET GO OF EXPECTATIONS: Just stop. Sit. Let go of the
routines and activities of your life. Don't expect anything. Be curious. Be open. Let yourself be surprised.
As with meditation, you can't do a retreat "right" or
"wrong." Don't get caught in comparing your experience
to anyone else's. Of course, you will judge; you will compare. Pay attention to this. "Ah, isn't this judging and
comparing interesting?"

REENTER AND RE-CREATE YOUR WORLD: Returning
from retreat can be challenging. I recall some Zen retreats where at the end of the seven-day period, desserts
were served and there was a celebratory atmosphere.
Yet I wanted and needed to be quiet, to connect quietly
with people. I felt shy, vulnerable, and exposed. I was
usually lured in by the prospect of a piece of chocolate cake
but then quietly left and returned to my own quiet space.

I can also remember coming home from retreats and feeling
that quietude instantly disappear as I returned to my ordinary life.
I would sometimes feel judgmental and grumpy. Then, if lucky, I
would catch myself and be open enough to say, "Oh, isn't this an
interesting story."

In short, be gentle with yourself as you return to your life after retreat. Accept the people, the problems, the joy and discomfort, just as if you were in retreat. Also, accept your annoyance, impatience, and judgments (about yourself and others). To bring the spirit of your retreat to your life means to accept whatever comes up, not that each moment of your life will or should be henceforth serene. Welcome back to the world!

At the same time, when you feel annoyed or impatient, see if you can bring your "retreat mind" into the situation. Notice the feelings, pause, and learn from whatever state of mind arises.

GENEROSITY: GIVING THE GIFT OF FEARLESSNESS

Generosity is an antidote to fear. When you practice generosity toward yourself and others, fear loosens its grip. Generosity in this case means gratitude for and acceptance of who we are and what is. After all, it takes less energy to relax and release than it does to clench and hold on, or to attempt to control or manipulate others or the environment. The result is greater accomplishment with less effort.

The fact that everything has been given to us is so obvious that it can be difficult to fathom. Our hands and eyes, our body and mind — all gifts! The air we breathe, the water we drink, the stars in the sky — gifts. If we can really let this feeling of awe envelop us, it shifts nearly everything that we can so easily take for granted about our work, our relationships, and our lives.

It's often difficult for us to meet our challenges and problems with generosity, and to express gratitude for painful experiences, large or small. To give just a simple example, when I encounter a long, slow line at the grocery story, I often think of one of my favorite quotes by calligrapher Kazuaki Tanahashi: "If you learn to enjoy waiting, you don't have to wait to enjoy." You can practice generosity with everything in daily life — and doing so can help you cope with traffic delays, cancelled flights, and coffee spills on your clean shirt, as well as those major emotional and physical challenges that strike unexpectedly.

Even more difficult to fathom, not only do we receive the gifts of life and beauty from the world, but we give these gifts! We are not separate from our body and mind, from the air and water, and from the stars. In a mysterious, practical, and essentially unknowable way, we are involved in creating everything. Every breath, every thought, and every action we take is both a gift and an act of generosity.

Practicing generosity in our daily lives, in our work, and in our relationships is not easy or simple. Giving that is self-centered or self-serving is merely another form of fear. But giving our full caring and attention to someone, without expecting anything in return, is an act of generosity. Real generosity requires that we open our hearts and allow ourselves to be curious and vulnerable and accepting. Gratitude says yes to all facets of life, even the difficult ones, which also leaves us open to experiencing more joy. The generosity of acceptance feels like doing less, but it brings us more. It is amazingly regenerative.

During an "Accomplishing More By Doing Less" retreat, one of the participants was a recently retired physics professor, whom I'll call Michael. For the previous fifteen years Michael's work had been his primary focus, and he generally averaged twelve-hour workdays. During lunch on the second day of the three-day workshop, he asked me, "When is the theme of this workshop, how to get more done by doing less, going to become clear?" His impatience was obvious. I responded that I thought that everything we were doing in the workshop focused on ways of exploring how to do less.

When we began the next session that afternoon, I suggested to Michael and to the group that often we get distracted by searching for answers. Sometimes, slowing down and being generous with ourselves can create space for the right questions to emerge, often slowly, allowing us to go deeper in our lives and open doors to new ways of approaching and resolving thorny issues.

The next morning, the third and last day of the retreat, I could see tears in Michael's eyes as he began to speak about an insight. He had come to the workshop wanting to better utilize and prioritize his time as he was leaving his busy professional life. What he came to understand, through doing less and experimenting with being generous with himself, was that what really mattered in his life at this time was healing some of the gaps in his relationships with his two grown daughters.

Finding composure and acting with clarity and resolve, right in the midst of your fears, is a form of generosity that in Buddhism is referred to as "giving the gift of fearlessness." I remember several years ago someone approached me after I had given a talk to an audience of several hundred people. He said that he noticed that my hands were shaking as I was speaking, yet my voice and body seemed clear and calm. I responded that this was exactly how I felt — shaky, filled with fear, and, at the same time, clear and calm.

Experiment with the practice of generosity. Give your attention, your caring, and your curiosity to those you live with and work with, without expecting anything in return. Take it on as an actual practice. Say yes, to yourself and to others. Notice and write about your acts of generosity as well as the generosity of others.

LIST YOUR FEARS AND ACT

In itself, increasing awareness of fear through meditation helps alleviate fear. But taking concrete action to address our fears is a necessary step as well.

Try This Exercise

On a sheet of paper, make a list of your fears. Label one column "My Fears," and list all the fears you can think of. Be as specific as possible. For example, fear of losing your job, fear of not having enough money, fear of speaking in front of an audience, fear of not meeting a soul mate, fear of not having children, fear of losing a loved one to a terminal illness, fear of not finding a profession about which to feel passionate. Write down all of the things you are afraid of in your life.

Then label the adjacent column "Next Actions." In this column list any concrete actions that would directly address or quiet these fears. For example, if you fear losing your job, write down why. If it's because of your own poor performance (or someone's perception of your performance), your next action could be to ask for feedback from people who work around you regarding how you could be more effective in your job. Then, follow up on that advice. Take a class to develop communication or presentation skills, or meet with a coach. If you fear being fired for reasons you can't control (say, company-wide cutbacks), then your next action could be to start a new job search, now. Fears about seemingly elusive goals — such as finding a soul mate — can sometimes lend themselves to concrete steps. If you're just not meeting the right people, find new ways and places to meet them. If you harbor self-defeating attitudes about yourself as a mate, take action! Practice a combination of daily self-awareness and self-acceptance.

Though we can lessen fear, we can't truly eliminate fear from our life. We will always be challenged to take the important and courageous steps to become more aware of, familiar with, and friends with fear. The practices outlined here can help you do that. By learning to continually identify and lessen your fear, the basic ground of your life can shift — from a life of busyness (which is often the result of trying to escape facing our fears) to a life of deepening, one that's more aware, calm, composed, and self-accepting. With this deeper sense of composure, we can become much more adept at accepting and helping others. That is the highest form of generosity and perhaps the highest form of expression for a human being.

CHAPTER 5

ASSUMPTIONS

According to neuroscience, even before events happen the brain
has already made a prediction about what is most likely to happen,
and sets in motion the perception, behaviors, emotions, physiologic
responses and interpersonal ways of relating that best fit with what
is predicted. In a sense, we learn from the past what to predict for the
future and then live the future we expect.

— Regina Pally, *The Predicting Brain*

WE ARE ALWAYS MAKING PREDICTIONS and assumptions. In fact, we
are generally brilliant assumption makers. When walking down
stairs, we trust the next steps will be there. When driving a car, we
make hundreds of assumptions regarding the functioning of our car
and the behavior of other drivers. If we're reading and letters are
missing from a word, we can effortlessly fill in the missing letters. We
can look at a person's face and, usually with accuracy, assess their
emotional state. To function in everyday life, we are required to make
tons of assumptions about the causes of events and what will happen
next. But predictions and assumptions are often wrong. And when
things go wrong, and conflicts ensue, the fastest and most effective
solution is often to identify and let go of any false assumptions.

For instance, many years ago when I was a young Zen student living at Green Gulch Farm in California, a problem arose among the residents: a sliding wooden door at the entrance of the student living area was regularly being left open. As a result, cold Pacific Ocean winds would sweep in and chill our shared living space. Announcements were made at least a half dozen times at community work meetings reminding people to keep this door shut. But it was continually found open, and over time this became a surprisingly divisive issue. People grew emotional, blaming and pointing fingers. How could Zen students not remember to close a door? How could they exhibit such thoughtlessness for their fellow students? In the midst of one these tense meetings, Sierra, the farm's pet golden retriever, opened the door from the outside, entered the living space, and joined the group. Of course, Sierra didn't also close the door. Everyone laughed. No one knew that Sierra had the dexterity to open a sliding wooden door. The group's false assumptions had nearly led to an all-out battle.

Admittedly this story has a comical ending. It's a rare case when saying "the dog did it" was actually true.

However, many conflicts are based on assumptions or incomplete understandings. This is often the case when we make assumptions about other people's motivations: we may interpret someone's actions entirely differently depending on what we infer about their feelings for us, their agenda, their personal history, their religious beliefs, their work ethic, and so on.

For instance, several years ago, while I was CEO of Brush Dance, I was working in our company booth at a stationery trade show in New York City. We were one among hundreds of booths in the Javits Center, which was a hive of activity, full of thousands of people. I was standing at the front of our booth greeting prospective buyers, artists, and others during a particularly packed and busy afternoon. One of my representatives, Charley, approached me

from the right and began a conversation. As we were speaking, a
buyer from a large bookstore chain approached me from the left.
I turned to her and we began speaking.

About a year after this event, during a phone call with Charley,
I noticed that he was not his usual friendly self. I asked him if he was
feeling alright. He told me that he was angry with me and had been
upset for the past year. He felt that I had "dropped him" and been
rude and dismissive during our meeting at the Javits Center. For all
these months he'd felt I had slighted him by favoring a person who
seemed to have more power and to offer a financial opportunity.

When he told me this, I apologized. I hadn't meant to insult
or hurt him, and I had no idea I had done so. In the moment, I had
been caught up in the show's hectic atmosphere and did not mean
anything when I turned to talk to someone else. Charley had
made an assumption about my intentions and had harbored hurt
feelings for an entire year. If I hadn't asked him about his feelings,
and if he hadn't honestly told me their cause, our relationship —
both business and personal — might never have recovered.

This incident highlights two important things. One is that
when we make assumptions about someone else's behavior, we can
almost never see or guess the whole truth. It's hard enough, in fact,
for us to know our own motivations for doing things! Perhaps at
the Javits Center I did unintentionally "drop" my conversation
with Charley, but I did not do so consciously or for the reasons he
assumed. I meant neither to insult him nor to communicate his
level of importance to me. He took my actions personally, when
they weren't meant that way at all. This experience is a good lesson about looking more deeply at our assumptions, especially our
tendency to overpersonalize interactions when doing so is neither
appropriate nor helpful.

But as importantly, Charley would never have known his
assumption was false if he hadn't told me honestly why he felt hurt.

We need to test or verify our assumptions as well. If Charley had blown off my question about how he was doing, then one small, unintentional slight might have grown into something much worse. This is why it is important to tell people when they have hurt us, and to do so sooner rather than later, and to tell them in a way that they can hear it. If a conflict is based on false assumptions, then we might cause more damage through our silence than through the incident itself.

The rest of this chapter offers practical techniques for reducing false assumptions and increasing mutual understanding. Many times, our false assumptions are based on our fears of what people think, so the first two categories of the Less Manifesto, fear and assumptions, work together. Addressing our fears and assumptions allows us to increase our trust of others, to increase productivity in the workplace, to improve harmony in our families and communities, and even to bring more peace into the world. Less fear and fewer false assumptions help us unclutter our emotions and thoughts, integrate the rational and intuitive parts of our personalities, and improve our ability to love others and ourselves. While love and trust may not seem to have much to do with productivity, without them nothing much gets accomplished.

UNCOVERING OUR OWN ASSUMPTIONS

Living is easy with eyes closed,
misunderstanding all you see.

— The Beatles

A seven-year-old girl is riding in a car with her mother. As they turn onto the highway on-ramp the girl blurts out to her mother, "Mama, mama, where are all the idiots?" The mother looks puzzled and asks her daughter, "What are you talking about?"

"When Daddy is driving there are always lots of idiots in other cars," she explains.

What assumptions do you make about other people — on the phone, at work, or on the highway? Is the world full of idiots and selfish people or warmhearted, caring people who pretty much want the same things you want? Then, what assumptions do you make about yourself: What kind of person do you think you are? How do you expect you will show up, act, and respond in any given situation?

In fact, do you even realize what your assumptions are? By definition, assumptions are attitudes, opinions and expectations we take for granted. Our perspective seems true, as if it reflects reality, so we don't question it. I often tell my coaching clients, when it comes to understanding human experience and consciousness, to imagine that every person lives on his or her own unique planet. We can cause a good deal of confusion when we assume that everyone lives on the same planet we live on. We cannot know another person's experience. We cannot truly know how someone else feels, what they think, or what their aspirations are. By the same token, others can't know everything that ticks inside of us. The best way to understand others is to ask them: "How *do* you feel about this? How do you see or understand this situation? What is your perspective?" The best way for others to understand us is to tell them: "*This* is how I feel." This may sound self-evident, but this type of honest, open communication is not engaged in enough.

If we want to make fewer false assumptions, and have more composure and effectiveness in our lives, we have to start by understanding ourselves. The meditation exercises in chapter 4 are an important way to do this. Another equally important strategy, which is the focus of this chapter, is talking and listening to others. Asking for regular and honest feedback from others is a valuable way to unearth our false assumptions and transform them into understanding. Is the way we think of ourselves the same as the way we are perceived: in the workplace, on a team, as a leader or collaborator, at home with loved ones? Just opening our ears and listening with calmness can help us learn to hear criticism in a way that does not immediately trigger defensiveness. Feedback is one of the simplest and most direct ways to measure whether our results match our goals. If we mean to be helpful, do people experience us that way? If not, why not? This kind of feedback can help us see our own false assumptions (about ourselves, about the needs of others) and fix self-defeating behaviors that often undermine our efforts and relationships.

It's surprising how doing this can make us not only more efficient at work and successful in our relationships but also a lot happier in general. Listening to another person's experience (whether it's about us or not) is a chance to understand ourselves and them, to grasp where they're coming from and what *motivates them* in their interactions with us. In this kind of environment, everyone's assumptions get tested and either confirmed or discarded. We decrease our tendency to jump to conclusions; we increase real understanding; and more understanding leads to greater productivity and results.

CLEANING MURKY WATER

A consultant I know described a recent assignment at a financial services organization. The moment he walked into the office, he could feel the high level of frustration, the result of posturing between the sales managers and the production staff. He said to the company's CEO, "The atmosphere here feels like a fish tank that has very dirty water. Do you ever think about cleaning out the tank and putting fresh water in?" The CEO had no idea what the consultant was referring to. Often we get so accustomed to the environment we are in — as organizations and individuals — that we don't notice when the "water is dirty." If we do notice, we may make any number of assumptions: that someone besides us dirtied the water; that there's no way to improve the situation or clean the tank; that our actions won't help; that cleaning it is not our problem or responsibility. This CEO did notice, once it was pointed out to him, and he took a series of steps — working with an executive coach and an outside consultant, improving communication among managers — that made concrete positive changes.

However, asking for and being open to feedback is not easy. Last summer I participated in a five-day leadership workshop in which my leadership skills would be observed and critiqued. Before the workshop, I was asked to get at least five people to fill out a written form describing my leadership performance and effectiveness. I did everything I could to avoid this. I procrastinated like crazy, telling the instructor that I was not managing a team during this time in my life and that I didn't think it appropriate to ask my coaching or consulting clients for this type of feedback. The instructor didn't blink: he said the feedback was a fundamental part of the leadership course, and that I could ask friends, colleagues, or former clients to fill out the form. Just before the program began, I relented and asked six different people (my wife, two coaching colleagues, and three former clients) for feedback. In the end, I was stunned by how useful this feedback was and the difference it made in working to develop myself as a leader, both specifically for the topics I knew would be addressed at the workshop and just generally in my life. Sometimes the feedback was difficult to hear (and I would register a mental "yes, but . . ." as I read); however, it was all thought-provoking and helpful in showing me ways to improve my leadership skills.

In fact, we are receiving feedback all the time — from our friends, partners, children, and colleagues. But we also tend to interpret any feedback so that it fits our preexisting assumptions and beliefs: about ourselves, about the givers of the feedback, and about the culture around us. The difficult challenge is to hear feedback without becoming defensive, and then, when necessary, to change ourselves and our assumptions in light of it. Soliciting feedback from trusted and truthful allies is one of the most targeted ways to do less and accomplish more.

> The difficult challenge is to hear feedback without becoming defensive, and then, when necessary, to change ourselves and our assumptions in light of it.

It is important to distinguish between constructive feedback and thoughtless, purely negative feedback that can block understanding or openness to change. Carefully consider whom you ask for feedback, and at least initially, make sure to choose people you really trust, those whom you know have your best interests at heart. Also, don't get feedback from just one person and stop; try to get several opinions, particularly to get clarity about complex, difficult issues. Remember, we each come from our own perspective, and even a well-meaning opinion is just one opinion; sometimes we need numerous opinions to fully understand problems and find fresh, effective solutions.

GETTING FEEDBACK

Getting effective feedback increases our knowledge about ourselves. It is part of the human condition that there are limits to our self-awareness. Precisely because we are inside ourselves — no matter how constantly we self-assess — we can lose perspective on how we function in the world and how others see us. Granted, sometimes the very word "feedback" can make our stomachs knot up, but when it's offered honestly and received openly, feedback can easily improve interactions with others and decrease false assumptions all around.

How you ask for feedback can affect the feedback you receive. Rather than posing a negative question — "What am I doing wrong?" — an effective way to get constructive feedback is to ask a positive question: "What (or how) can I do better?" This is a terrific question to ask of people you work with — those who report to you and those to whom you report. It's also a great question to ask of your children, your spouse, parents, and friends. To get more specific feedback, make your question more specific, and include your desires and goals: "I would like to achieve [X]. What can I do better in [these areas]?" At root, though, it's such a simple request, "What can I do better?" And it's effective because implicit in the question is your desire to improve and, either directly or indirectly, help the other person. Another version, one perhaps more appropriate to a spouse or family member than a coworker, I first heard asked by Vietnamese Zen teacher Thich Nhat Hanh: "Please tell me, how can I love you better?" The wonderful challenge is then to open-heartedly deliver on those requests.

I recognize that these "simple" questions are not so simple. If we don't interact effectively with certain individuals or in certain situations, we tend to rationalize this in any number of ways, and then we can cling tenaciously to this armor of assumptions. We jump to conclusions and then respond in counterproductive ways that seem immutable or fated. But becoming aware of these assumptions, and being open to changing them, can be nothing short of transformative.

Asking for feedback is the first step, but the important next step is listening, just listening (which I'll discuss more below). This is often harder than asking for feedback, but it's essential if you want continued and helpful feedback in the future. When someone talks, do not argue or explain why the feedback, or the person's perspective, is incorrect or unfair. Just listen, make sure you understand the feedback fully, and then thank the person. Remember, as hard as it is to listen to feedback, it can be equally hard to give honest criticism. The appropriate response to sincere feedback, whether you agree with it or not, is, "Thank you, I appreciate what you've said, and I will think about these things." The next step is to do just that: without berating or beating up on yourself, or the person giving the feedback, use the feedback to consider what assumptions you should discard as false, and what direction or attitude would lead to a more satisfying result.

Many years ago when I was running the publishing company Brush Dance, I hired a team of consultants to help me with marketing and overall strategy issues. One day the consultants pulled me aside and asked if I realized that many of my employees were afraid to speak openly with me. They said the people who worked with me did not feel I was listening or responding to their concerns. I was completely stunned. "Me? They don't feel they can talk to me?" I was operating under a completely different assumption — in this case, a falsely positive one — about how I was perceived by my employees.

As a midlevel employee myself in several previous jobs, I had experienced what is sometimes referred to as "CEO disease" — the communication gap that exists between a person in power and those around that person. As a CEO myself at Brush Dance, I was humbled at one time to find out that my employees didn't feel I was listening to them and didn't feel safe to disagree with me. To address this, the consultants had Brush Dance's twelve employees anonymously fill out surveys rating my leadership skills. Using this, I obtained lots of information regarding my leadership strengths and weaknesses; I had a number of heart-to-heart conversations with people in all departments and at all levels; and I made changes in my communication style that had a positive impact on employee morale and the business's performance. It was remarkable how clear the link was.

Feedback in Practice: Looping and Dipping

Listening is normally considered passive, but when we ask for feedback, we need to practice active listening. A friend who teaches mediation skills to attorneys has developed a technique for this he calls "looping" — which is summarizing what another person has said to confirm that there is understanding. Typically, whenever we receive criticism, our immediate reaction is to formulate a response or defend ourselves, and when we do this, we stop listening. Instead, when receiving feedback, practice looping, in which you focus only on actively and accurately listening to what is said, and then summarizing it back once the person is finished. Once you're done summarizing, ask: "Did I hear what you said? Did I leave out anything important?" This tool can go far toward increasing our compassion for the other person, and honoring that person's painful emotions, especially if we are the cause of their negative feelings.

From the other side of the table, so to speak, "dipping" is the practice of being aware of your feelings as someone is "looping" what you said. As your words are being summarized, what is your emotional state? Are *you* listening from start to finish? You don't necessarily need to express what you are feeling, but "dipping" down into your feelings can add more information or help clarify next steps.

Now, put this into practice. Next week, either at work or at

home, ask at least one person in your close sphere for feedback on
a particular issue. At work, perhaps initially ask coworkers or
peers (rather than bosses or employees) for feedback on how you
can improve as a teammate and collaborator — are there other,
better ways you could contribute, listen, support others, or lead?
Pay careful attention both to what people say about you and to how
hard or easy it is for you to receive the feedback. Are you able
to listen actively and nondefensively? How do people respond to
your request, and do you think the way you asked affected their
responses? What did people say? Keep a list of their statements,
however casual, and at the end of the week, look them over all
together. Do you see any patterns, any surprises? Does the picture
they paint match your sense of self? If there are problems with
your work style, what action plan, even a private one, will you
undertake to make appropriate changes?

Alternatively, get feedback from one or two relatives or
friends. Ask them: How can I be a better spouse, sibling, or friend?
Then just listen. I think you will be amazed at how many of your
assumptions about yourself and others need adjusting. A wonderful surprise is that sometimes we find that people feel a lot more
positively about us than we think they do — so that some of
the assumptions we invariably need to change are the negative ones
we hold.

IDENTIFYING TRIGGERS

*If you are patient in one moment of anger,
you will escape one hundred years of sorrow.*

— Chinese proverb

One of my clients, Kathy, is the director of program development
for a major nonprofit organization. Kathy is in her midthirties,

astute, and ambitious, and she has had a successful career as a project manager in the corporate and nonprofit arenas. In a coaching session, she described leading a meeting in which her team was brainstorming ideas for new initiatives to serve a large potential client. In the midst of the meeting, Tom, a manager in his mid-fifties, raised his hand and stated that he didn't understand why they were spending so much time brainstorming.

Kathy was immediately "triggered." As Tom spoke, Kathy's body tightened and her face became red. She was overtaken by feelings of anger. She wanted to lash out at Tom but knew this was neither appropriate nor constructive. Then almost immediately her anger turned to self-doubt. She could feel herself losing her usual self-confidence. She felt much like a child in a woman's body. She wanted to cry but didn't.

Speaking about this event the next day, Kathy acknowledged a familiar pattern. When I asked what she had experienced during the meeting, she said, "I felt so unappreciated, challenged, and not seen by Tom." She acknowledged this is something she has experienced many times in her life.

I asked Kathy to close her eyes, relax, and take a few deep breaths. I asked her if she could recall similar feelings from an earlier time in her life. Immediately I could see tears in her eyes. She described when she was a little girl, around nine or ten years old. She was sitting at the dinner table with her family. Her father was expressing disapproval and disappointment with her grades in school. She felt unappreciated, almost invisible.

This is a classic example of being triggered. Someone says something, and our body suffers an almost chemical reaction. Initially, we may feel an overwhelming fight-or-flight response; our body tenses and our breath becomes shallow. Anger arises, followed by anxiousness or sadness or self-doubt. We freeze like a deer in the headlights — unable to respond well or appropriately to the situation at hand. Usually, what has happened is that we are caught in an old pattern, reacting to a long-gone event, often from childhood. We feel stuck, unable to respond in a different or more effective way, and unable to keep from reacting whenever we get triggered.

There are numerous ways we become triggered. When we say someone "pushes our buttons," we mean the same thing: we can't help but react to them, even when our reaction isn't appropriate. Triggers are based on false beliefs, assumptions, and predictions that we make and that make us unhappy and entrenched in hurt feelings. These can be survival patterns from past experiences, or habitual ways of responding we've acquired to protect ourselves.

Take a few moments to think about times when you are triggered; what are some specific situations? It can be liberating to become aware of the feeling of being triggered. With awareness, we can gain the ability to choose, at least to some degree, how to respond differently than we have in the past.

The first positive step to take when triggered is to name it: "Oh, I'm triggered." The next step is to create space and slow down. When we get triggered, it is best not to react or respond, since our strong emotions have more to do with an unresolved reaction to our past than with what just triggered our feelings. Take a break. Go to the restroom. Walk outside for a few minutes. At least pause and breathe deeply several times. This is not a good time to make decisions or give in to the way we habitually respond. You may want to tell the person you would like to think about what he or she is saying and arrange a time to meet and follow up. You can take this time to reflect on what has triggered you. You may also consider talking with a trusted friend or colleague to become more clear about your own triggers, to get a wider perspective. When you feel more clear, arrange to meet again. You might, or might not, choose to share with the person that you were triggered (the person probably felt it, anyway), but indicate that you are interested in hearing more. Then, listen to what is being said in this moment, which may be very different from your assumptions.

Pausing

An important and useful skill to learn is to recognize the signs of what happens to you when you are triggered. For example, do you feel yourself tightening in response to what someone says? Does your breathing become quicker, shallower? When this happens, you might experiment, if possible, with stepping back and becoming aware of your breath. The sensation of breathing can ground you, so you are not lost in the past.

You may also want to plan in advance an antidote you can rely on when you notice that you are triggered. One of the best I know of is simply to pause. Just stop. Take a moment to disengage from the situation, to slow down, and to be aware of your breath. When confronted with a particularly difficult situation, Pema Chödrön, an American Buddhist nun, offers this suggestion in her book *Practicing Peace in Times of War*: "If we pause and breathe in and out, then we can have the experience of timeless presence, of the inexpressible wisdom and goodness of our own minds. We can look out at the world with fresh eyes and hear things with fresh ears. In that pause...we can relax and open."

Another antidote you might explore is to intentionally say a word or phrase that can anchor or ground you when you notice you are triggered. For example you might say to yourself, "I'm here now." I know someone who says the words "peanut butter"

as a way to pause, diffuse the situation, and become more present
and aware. Some lightness or humor can be of great help during
difficult situations.

When we can pause, and for a moment decharge the personal
assumptions that flood in to fuel these challenging situations, we
can step beyond what closes us down. Then we might be surprised
by what we hear; we might discover that the other person has a
point of view that has a great deal to offer.

KNOW THYSELF

Beyond our assumptions lies a wider perspective that leads to
greater satisfaction and accomplishment. It is a positive circle in
both business and life: Trust lies at the heart of human relationships; human relationship lies at the heart of composure and satisfaction; composure and satisfaction lead to better results.

Think for a moment of people you trust and the qualities they
exhibit. What they say and do are almost always in alignment. They
probably keep their word. When their words and actions are not in
accord, they are quick to admit it and apologize. You just know they
have your best interests at heart. They can keep a confidence. You
know this partly because they do not gossip about others to you and
do not revel in others' downturns
when they relate them to you.

**Trust lies at the heart of human
relationships; human relationship
lies at the heart of composure
and satisfaction; composure and
satisfaction lead to better results.**

What I have often found surprising is that many more people are
trustworthy than conventional wisdom assumes. Thinking about the
hundreds of vendors and small companies that I have worked
with and relied upon over the years, I believe that when people are
treated with honesty and respect, they respond with honesty and
respect.

To Try

In your journal begin writing with the following open-ended sentences. Don't think about the task very much or self-edit before writing; just write and see what you can learn.

When I get triggered, I notice that _____.
When conflicts arise, I generally feel _____.
What works well for me when difficult emotions arise is

_____.

Also, try this: Whether in your journal or in conversation with a friend or mentor, identify a person who is challenging for you — what are your assumptions about this person? How do you or might you prepare for conversations with this person? What happens in your body when you think about speaking with this person?

SPEAKING UP: THE "NO FESTERING" RULE

In my work with corporate management teams, I've found that instituting a "no festering" rule can be a useful antidote to ward off false assumptions. As I've said, when we have a problem with someone and we don't talk to that person about it honestly and respectfully, our fears and resentments often fill the silence with false assumptions that can make the situation much worse than it really is.

I created this rule when I was CEO of Brush Dance. My chief operating officer, Janice, was a strong and competent woman, and though I valued her opinion, I did not always agree with it. Increasingly, though, she seemed to be uncomfortable around me. I often noticed her grimacing and sighing in my presence or just looking depleted. When we worked closely together, I noticed myself sometimes "walking on eggshells" around her. I did this when I perceived that she was feeling stress and seemed unhappy.

I assumed I must have done something that displeased her. My tendency was to avoid conflict and difficult conversations, and with her I tried to accentuate the positive even when that did not make good business sense and difficult issues had to be addressed.

Eventually, I realized we needed to fix this problem, for the health of the business and for our relationship. I obviously needed to be able to speak freely and openly with my COO. When I talked with Janice about what I was noticing and feeling, she was surprised at my assumptions. She told me that her stress and anxiety were a result of difficulties she was having at home, with her husband and teenage daughter. While I was relieved that I wasn't the cause of her stress, I was embarrassed that my false assumptions had made things worse. Because of my behavior, Janice said, she sometimes saw me as cold and avoiding her. She interpreted this to mean that I was not happy with *her* performance, and as a result she felt unappreciated for her work. Ah, more false assumptions.

This one conversation cleared the air, and we felt and functioned much better afterward as a result. By then, we had both spent so much energy worrying about the situation, that everything we did together had come to seem effortful and exhausting. This was a great example of doing more and accomplishing less!

After this, we agreed on a "no festering" rule: If either of us were making what could possibly (or at least probably) be assumptions about the other person, we would express these ideas and feelings immediately and have an open, respectful dialogue. This agreement worked well, our relationship improved, and our operating team functioned much more effectively.

This practice isn't just useful in the office; it can be effective at home or anywhere two humans are in relationship.

Here is a three-step approach to speaking up and identifying assumptions:

1. Identify an issue or a problem that you have with another
    person that you have not directly addressed and that is
    influencing your relationship. Often, we make assump-
    tions about another person's motivations. However, while
    we can observe and have opinions about someone's
    actions or behavior, we cannot completely know a per-
    son's motivations unless he or she tells us.

2. Initiate a conversation with that person, stating what you
    observe and how you feel. It's very important to be patient,
    calm, and respectful, rather than angry or judgmental. In
    this situation, seek merely to understand the situation bet-
    ter, not to necessarily resolve it in the way you'd like. Be
    particularly considerate if the subject matter is a tough one
    to approach. Ask if the person is willing to share his or her
    motivations, and if he or she has any questions or feelings
    about your behavior or motivations. Are your assumptions
    about the person's motivations and behavior correct? Did
    you learn anything that changed your thinking and under-
    standing and could lead to new behavior?

3. Depending on how the conversation went, agree on a "no
    festering" rule for the future. Make a pact to speak directly
    whenever issues and conflicts come up. For yourself, at
    least, you can always live by following a "no festering"
    rule. It's amazing how much mental busyness you'll avoid.

ASK FOR, AND OFFER, HELP

Tired of making assumptions or erroneously jumping to conclusions? Ask for help; don't assume you know.

Asking requires little effort and may lead to very big results.
Asking about a person's motivations or intentions can be flatter-
ing because it demonstrates genuine interest in the person as a

respected teammate, a cherished friend, a beloved partner, even an appreciated new acquaintance. Asking is such a powerful and overlooked skill that I present it here as a practice. As with most skills, some people are already highly adept at it, while others could gain significantly through practice and improvement.

In our culture, knowledge is power, but I would counter that not knowing is highly underrated. Or, stated differently, approaching life and relationships as one who is still learning is more effective than acting like someone who knows everything, someone with nothing to learn. Asking increases understanding, it opens a dialogue with others, and through it we can build unexpected connections. People are sometimes reluctant to ask, because asking makes us vulnerable, since it admits, to one degree or another, that there may be quite a bit we don't know.

Vulnerability caused by not knowing is a condition that all human beings have in common. It is one of our most unifying and precious traits, yet it seems we value it and show it all too little. I hope if you currently undervalue your vulnerability that you will reconsider that position. The funny thing is that when we're more vulnerable, we're more open to help from others. This can be key to maximizing the expertise and insight of others — and benefiting from their productivity.

How we ask and, indeed, the words we use, are tremendously important. Language plays an enormous role in forming our identity and in building relationships with others. Being clear with language results in better communication, more understanding, and greater results.

Experiment with practicing three specific types of effective asking: 1) make requests; 2) ask for the benefit of experience; and 3) make offers to help others.

Make Requests

This is a practice I often assign to coaching clients: During the next week, experiment with making direct requests. Begin sentences with words like, "I request that you..." and "Would you please..." These simple and direct words may not reflect the way many people traditionally speak. Making requests, however, can allow you to be more transparent — you are revealing and asking for what you want, and this is often touching and disarming to others. This is also a way to make the language we use in relating to others, especially the language we use in describing what we need and hope for, more precise and vivid.

Pay attention to when you make requests, and when you do not make requests. What stops you or gets in your way? How do you feel when you make a request? What happens when you don't make a request? Also, how do you usually respond to other people's requests? With a yes or no? If a yes, does it feel wholehearted or tepid?

But of course there is a shadow side to all of this "clarity" about what we are seeking. Sometimes when we are very clear about what we need from other people, we have to appreciate that they may not want to, or be able to, fulfill our request. Quite simply, we may be asking too much of them, or we may be asking in a way that does not make them want to respond positively. We have the power and the ability to ask for what we hope for or need. We either honor these needs or turn away from them. Once we ask, we also have the opportunity to learn from the way someone responds.

In short, all of the exercises and experiments suggested in this chapter (and throughout the book) need to be approached with a large dose of patience and a fundamental appreciation that human relationships can be immensely complicated. At the same time, it can be surprising what's possible, in a positive sense, right in the midst of this complexity. To quote the Kentucky writer-farmer Wendell Berry, "'Be joyful, though you've considered all the facts."

Ask for the Benefit of Experience

Recently, an artist was referred to me by an executive coaching colleague. She called me, introduced herself, and said: "I'm thinking of starting a greeting card business. How do I decide if this is right for me? Then what do I do after I make the decision? What are the first steps and the long-range issues I need to be aware of?" As the former CEO of a greeting card company, I had a pretty good sense of how to approach this question and felt honored that she asked for my advice. Knowing the business as well as I do, I quickly helped her develop a critical path for evaluating the key decisions involved in whether or not to start a card company, and at the same time I could lay out a framework for exploring related options for an artist — licensing, other forms of partnership arrangements, and so on. In a one-hour conversation I was able to distill many years of experience and provide this artist with a list of actions and ideas that could save her months of time and lots of money.

I was happy to answer this artist's questions, since just about everything I know about the greeting card business came from similar conversations I've had with others over the years — with representatives, manufacturers, printers, designers, lawyers, accountants, and other greeting card company owners. At the end, I also told the artist I was open to future conversations to mentor and guide her.

This phone conversation underscored for me how the practice

of asking can lead to positive results with little effort. What struck me most is that I didn't feel she was asking too much or being inappropriate in "picking my brain." Instead I felt delighted to be part of a stream of information sharing, which can be the most enjoyable and certainly one of the most efficient ways of conducting business.

As an exercise or experiment, practice doing this yourself by taking to lunch or coffee someone who is knowledgeable about a subject you want to learn more about.

Make Offers to Help

Though it might seem paradoxical, making offers to help others is actually a form of asking. If I offer to help you with your business plan, or offer to assist you with a birthday party for your child, I am asking your permission to enter into an agreement with you. It is important to be clear about the offers you are making and to affirm that your offer has been heard and accepted. It is also important to follow through appropriately on your offers. Making offers can be a way of moving toward a solution to a problem or creating a path or process that did not previously exist.

Practice making offers. Pay attention and mentally note the offers that you make. Notice any difficulty you may have making offers. Do you feel depleted or renewed by offering assistance? Occasionally, of course, both feelings may occur simultaneously, but focus on your dominant response. Would it be helpful to alter this typical response?

At the very least, all these forms of asking are rooted in the best of what makes us human. In addition, they go far toward helping us not jump to conclusions or make false, and usually quite unhelpful, assumptions.

In the Zen tradition, there is a famous dialogue between two leading teachers in sixth-century China, a time when Zen was flourishing. One teacher asked another: "What is the Way?" This is another way of asking — How can I live a happy, meaningful life? Or, How can I find real freedom? The other teacher responded, much to the first teacher's surprise, "Ordinary mind is the Way."

I find this to be a wonderful, encouraging answer, as well as a terrific way to cut through our ideas and assumptions. This was not the answer that was expected or assumed, then or now. Ordinary mind is the way. Just trusting, or returning to, our ordinary mind is the way to find happiness and meaning! To find satisfaction, composure, and results — we don't need anything extra, fancy, or special. We don't need to do or add more; we need to do less! We just need to let go of some of our assumptions, particularly our thinking that our freedom and happiness lie someplace else, or during some other time, or with some other mind. Instead, let's be guided by our inclusive, playful, mysterious, and plain ordinary minds.

CHAPTER 6

DISTRACTIONS

Beeped and pinged, interrupted and inundated, overloaded and hurried
— that's how we live today.... What's needed is a renaissance of
attention — a revaluing and cultivating of the art of attention to help us
achieve depth of thought and relations in this complex, high-tech time.

— Maggie Jackson, *New York Times*, June 22, 2008

Wisdom is the art of knowing what to overlook.

— William James

DISTRACTIONS AND INTERRUPTIONS are such a part of modern life
that we don't realize how hard it is to concentrate. We've almost
lost the ability to pay attention to the fact that we're not paying
close attention. Many neuroscientists, psychologists, and technology pundits believe that the distractions of our communication
technology are actually rewiring our brain's capacity to concentrate for any amount of time on one topic. For example, in a
much-discussed 2008 article in *The Atlantic*, "Is Google Making
Us Stupid?" Nicholas Carr, one of the leading thinkers on information technology, states, "And what the Net seems to be doing
is chipping away my capacity for concentration and contemplation.
My mind now expects to take in information the way the Net dis-
tributes it: in a swiftly moving stream of particles. Once I was a

scuba diver in the sea of words. Now I zip along the surface like a guy on a Jet Ski." This article generated lots of buzz because Carr questioned whether the utterly familiar yet, in truth, newly introduced medium of the Internet was itself profoundly influencing our ability to think and to process information.

What *are* distractions? Are they that bad? Is there any going back to the perhaps romantic era when we had more time to think, focus, and do one thing at a time? Can anything be done to reduce distractions, especially at work, since by their very definition distractions are usually unexpected, often urgent, and almost always unavoidable? And have we become smitten with our distractions of choice — texting, instant messaging, twittering, listening to iPods, checking email, reading RSS feeds, checking the news on the Internet? Also, in truth, many of us like distractions and interruptions. They're fun, even necessary, and so is multitasking. If we did just one thing at a time, wouldn't we be bored and unhappy and not accomplish very much? In a funny way, focusing seems like yesterday's way of doing things.

This chapter will show why too many distractions and being drawn in multiple directions create distractedness — the opposite of engaged, responsive, productive attention. In other words, the opposite of focus, which is not and most likely never will be yesterday's way of doing things no matter how busy we get. Focus is not only a necessary, safe, effective, and satisfying way to achieve goals; focus is also enjoyable.

GREAT, AND NOT-SO-GREAT, DISTRACTIONS

There are two primary types of distractions: those that draw us in multiple directions at once, resulting in confusion and an inability to complete a thought or action, and those that provide mental relaxation, offering small "breaks" that support intense focus and effort. Clearly, we want less of the former and more of the latter. This chapter primarily focuses on how to lessen the undermining distractions — the pull of conflicting internal and external voices, and a lack of focus and clarity, which results in priorities and intentions being out of alignment with actions. Strangely, we rarely think of distractions as good, but they can be: for instance, listening to music while working can sometimes support our focus, not take away from it. Also, meditation, retreats, mindfulness practice, and breathing techniques aren't usually considered distractions per se, but in this sense they are. They distract us from our usual patterns and habits. At the same time, they inform us so we can work better and live better.

However, we all know what distractedness, in the undermining sense, feels like. Typically, when we're doing a dozen things at once, constantly stopping and starting, and never quite finishing anything, we feel we are working very hard, but our results aren't commensurate with our efforts. Whenever this happens, we feel discouraged. After all, when we are working nearly nonstop, multitasking, and giving our maximum effort to everyone, we want praise and satisfaction to follow. We want to be viewed as exemplary. However, even though our intentions are good, when we jam-pack our days with activities, and stretch ourselves thin dealing with myriad demands — and crises — we usually reach the end of the day feeling less productive and effective, as well as more exhausted, depleted, and slightly depressed.

> We need to learn how to turn each day into an opportunity not only for sustained productivity but for composure and enjoyment, which can actually lead to more sustained productivity.

This is an all-too-common scenario, one that leaves us addled and wondering how long we can sustain this craziness. We approach work as if it were a blitzkrieg (which is German for "lightning war"). Instead, we need to learn how to turn each day into an opportunity not only for sustained productivity but for composure and enjoyment, which can actually lead to more sustained productivity.

MANAGING DISTRACTIONS

In *The Mindful Brain*, renowned child psychiatrist and educator Daniel Siegel writes: "We can actually focus our minds in a way that changes the structure and function of the brain throughout our lives.... [B]eing aware of the present moment without grasping onto judgments offers a powerful path toward both compassion and inner well-being. This is what science verifies and what has been taught over thousands of years of practice."

Heike Bruch and Sumantra Ghoshal — in their well-titled article "Beware the Busy Manager" in the *Harvard Business Review* — cite a study that found that 90 percent of managers squander their time in ineffective activities, and only 10 percent spend time in a committed, purposeful, and reflective manner.

"The smallest proportion of managers we studied — around 10% — were both highly energetic and highly focused.... Purposeful managers tend to be more self-aware than most people.... They pick their goals — and also their battles — with far more care than other managers do."

As we all know, some days are just hopelessly busy, with tasks taking you in many different directions, but the number of those days can be reduced. We can never eliminate distractions, but we can lessen them and manage the ones that remain so that they don't drain our focus and energy. This certainly improves our sense of satisfaction and effectiveness, since we maximize "results" while minimizing effort. To start, we need the intention to be more composed in order to experience more composure. Composure and focus aren't achieved just by lowering the number of tasks that need our attention. More important is how we prioritize the tasks before us, as well as the quality of attention we bring to those tasks.

What are some of the specific actions of the 10 percent of focused and energetic managers?

- They schedule regular "think time" and reflective time into their days.
- They keep disruptive inflow of information to a minimum by responding to emails and phone calls only at certain times of the day.
- They have well-developed strategies for reducing stress levels.
- They are thoughtful and strategic about the number of meetings they schedule and attend.

Work "Inside Out," Not "Outside In"

The study cited in the *Harvard Business Review* also found that less effective managers worked in a way that it described as "from the outside in." These managers tend to feel overly impacted by, and overly responsive to, external conditions and situations — they feel distracted and constrained by job descriptions, bosses, and peers. Less effective managers tend to be more easily thrown off their task and purpose by changing circumstances. They often don't use focusing mechanisms (like mindfulness or meditation) and as a result display less strength and clarity in their thoughts. They don't pare down distractive energies around them because they incorrectly believe they can't. They don't have a positive sense of their own power. This type of dysfunctional behavior is much easier to engage in than we think. It's worth honestly reflecting on our own choices and examining the way we manage distractions to see if we're doing so as effectively as we could.

On the other hand, the study said that more focused and effective managers work from the "inside out." They are clear about what needs to be achieved and are more skillful managing or adjusting their environments to achieve it. These managers have a clear sense of their priorities and continually guide their efforts toward their larger purpose. Instead of letting external circumstances constrain their aims, they coalesce the support and resources they need, and positively influence people, in order to achieve their goals. They have a strong sense of self but somehow are neither authoritarian nor ego driven. Perhaps most important, they make fellow workers feel very good about themselves and their contribution. Though they are themselves high achievers, these manager-leaders convey their respect for the distinctive talents of others.

This may sound like some dream manager, but effective managers really do these things. Think of managers you admire and most like to work with; they no doubt share some or all of these traits. Their increased effectiveness and productivity is the result of the way they approach their work and focus everyone's energy, especially their own.

In the world of work, we are often rewarded for displaying lots of energy, sometimes more so than for displaying focus. But in the long run, energy by itself doesn't equal effectiveness or lead to success. When we confuse sheer activity, and certainly frenetic activity, with productivity, we increase our energy and movement, and our busyness, without achieving what we want or meeting objectives.

STRATEGIES FOR REDUCING DISTRACTIONS

Constant distraction in our lives has become accepted and almost even fashionable. Just do one thing? How boring, how indulgent. Multitasking is cool; it shows we're needed, active, popular, skilled. But imagine driving without being on the telephone, eating, or putting on makeup. Imagine enjoying the sensory experience of walking through a city without talking on the phone. Then we would be engaged in the moment and entertained by our surroundings: by the faces of the passersby, by the colors and shapes of the trees, by the architecture. What might it feel like to work without the interruption of emails? To listen to someone else without already thinking about our response?

Here are five practices that can be useful tools in reducing distraction or frenetic activity and cultivating focus and concentration. They are surprisingly easy to implement and, almost before you know it, can become positive addictions.

1. Appreciate Impermanence

I saw a cartoon in a recent *New Yorker* magazine in which two people were finishing their dinners at a Chinese restaurant and had just opened their fortune cookies. One fortune read, "You are going to die."

If you let this fact sink in — that life is short, and we all die — it can actually act as a powerful motivating force to help maintain focus and priorities. Everything changes and is impermanent, so are we fully present and making the most of this fleeting moment? Are we fully aware of what we are doing? Appreciating impermanence clarifies priorities, and it helps us identify any frenetic, shallow, and ineffective activities we're being distracted by. We see clearly the things that exhaust us and distract us from experiencing the blessing and opportunity of each particular day.

In Zen practice it is often said that the span of our lives is like a dew drop on a leaf — beautiful, precious, and extremely short-lived. Life is remarkably unpredictable. Whatever you want to accomplish, whatever is important to you, do it, and do it now — with as much grace, intensity, and sense of ease as you can muster. None of us knows what life will bring. At any moment, everything we take for granted can change. We must be careful not to dwell on impermanence constantly, to the point that we become paralyzed with fear of loss, but we can use an awareness of change on a deep and wise level to focus our priorities and increase our appreciation of the sheer beauty of existence.

2. Clarify Aspirations and Create Next Steps

As you did in the fear exercise in chapter 4, make two lists. Title the first one "Aspirations, Plans, and Projects." Title the column next to this "Next Steps," and list concrete action steps toward implementation of each aspiration, plan, or project. What is the very first action required toward completing each item, and the step after that and the one after that? In the popular book *Getting Things Done*, productivity improvement expert David Allen describes the relief that people experience just by listing "next steps" in relation to incomplete projects. The act of identifying clear actions can have a freeing effect and make you feel that you're making progress (sometimes when mired in setbacks and resistance, project management minutiae, or office politics, this is not so easy to believe). It can be daunting having many projects hanging over your head, so this helps clarify the actions needed to move each project toward completion.

3. Retrain Pavlov's Dog

We react to email and phone calls the way Pavlov's dog reacted to a bell: we come running at once, tongues wagging. Instead, when approaching the daily onrush of emails, phone calls, and other attention "grabbers," try these habit diffusers and attention refocusers.

EMAILS

Learn to check your email only two or three times per day — say, at the middle and end of your day, or at the beginning, middle, and end. Granted, sometimes this isn't realistic. Sometimes we have truly time-sensitive matters to resolve, and we absolutely must read and reply immediately. But these situations are probably fewer than we think, and this type of behavior can be the exception rather than the rule. Actually, despite the prevailing belief that we live in a world where everyone expects quick, near-instantaneous responses, this isn't true. Most people don't need responses right away; they just get used to it. If you are a constant email checker, practice checking email only once an hour, then once every two hours, until you are down to only three times a day. What you will find is that in nearly every case, this satisfies everyone's communication needs, and it eliminates a major distraction from your life.

Phone Calls

As with email, learn to respond to phone calls or messages only two or thee times per day. Like changing any habit, learning this new behavior takes patience and some repatterning; give yourself a week at least. What you do also depends on your communication needs, but commit to different behavior. Let your message service do its job, so you can do yours. Retrain yourself not to always respond to the ring of the telephone or the vibration of the cell phone. This way, you control your interactions; they don't control you.

Think Time

Schedule think time and reflection time at the beginning and end of each day. This could include a full meditation, or perhaps just silent, focused thoughtfulness over a cup of coffee or tea, while taking a robust walk, or while still lying in bed first thing in the morning. In any case, commit to giving yourself this daily gift of a few moments to sit quietly and gather your thoughts. These can be some of the most pleasurable, precious, and practical moments of the day. They can help to reframe your focus and energy in unexpected ways.

4. Savor Borrowed Time

Borrowed time is a brief moment when we do nothing; we just breathe and smell the sweetness of the air, think briefly about the task we just completed or are about to start; or we listen to the birds flying, our heartbeat, or the conversations around us (without participating in them). These refreshing bits of time can be just a minute or two long, and they can happen many times throughout the day if we let them. They are, quite simply, daydreaming, but we shouldn't view them as guilty indulgences. One helpful result of engaging in the more disciplined practice of meditation or mindfulness is that it makes us more relaxed about "do-nothing" time. The quietude is familiar; all of these practices become the pause that refreshes.

A more advanced and powerfully effective practice is to see your entire life as borrowed time. Imagine, for a moment, that you have died and now have a chance to return to this life. Now what? What would you do differently? How would the quality of your decisions and actions be influenced? This exercise and practice, if fully embraced, can support and enhance focus.

> **A more advanced and powerfully effective practice is to see your entire life as borrowed time. Imagine, for a moment, that you have died and now have a chance to return to this life. Now what?**

5. Create Your Own Toolkit for Reducing Stress

Experiment with beginning each day, or most days, with meditation practice. Explore routines and rituals to center and relax during the day. Just breathing deeply and from the diaphragm three or four times, several times a day, can be a great start. Commit to stopping: notice the warm power of the sun or the sound of the freezing rain; smile; drink a glass of water; close your eyes for a minute or two; stretch your arms and legs, giving your neck and shoulders or hands a mini-massage; or get up from your desk to chat with a colleague down the hall. It can be any activity that refreshes and makes you pause from the whirlwind of activity you may have (unconsciously) gotten yourself into. If you work at a computer for much of the day, consider setting a timer to remind you to stop and stretch at regular intervals.

ENVISIONING SUCCESS

If you weren't so distracted by the busyness of your life, what is it you would want to accomplish? Sometimes distractions overwhelm us because we haven't visualized our highest priority. So, in this exercise, you will imagine what, in a perfect world, you'd like to achieve and become. However, don't be "realistic." Imagine what you'd do if you had all the resources you needed — no constraints of money, resources, respect, or time. What if there were no excuses? Then what? What do you want to accomplish?

Sit down, close your eyes, and take a few deep breaths. Relax your body; put your attention on your breath. Breathe all the way in, and all the way out.

See the calendar in front of you with today's date. Now, see the days unfolding forward day by day, week by week. Watch the days move forward until it is today's date three years from today. See the day and the year.

Picture where you are and what you are doing, three years from now. Again, don't worry about constraints of resources — let yourself imagine freely. See the place, the details of your surroundings. See yourself engaged in work you love. See the people you are working with. These are the kinds of people you really enjoy working with and who help you realize your most productive and creative endeavors. Imagine that your muscles and bones and brain feel relaxed.

Now visualize a magazine or journal that you hold in high regard. Imagine that there is an article in this magazine about you and the work you have been doing recently. See the headline of the article and imagine the contents. What does it say that you are doing? What is the innovation or breakthrough you developed that is the focus of the article?

Now see yourself on the cover of the magazine. How do you look? Are you smiling with sincerity or perhaps looking serious and confident? What is the headline describing you and your accomplishment? What emotions arise in you as you observe yourself?

As you complete the reading of this imaginary article, begin to bring your attention back to your breathing and body. Slowly and gently return to this day and this place and open your eyes.

Write down what you envisioned:

- What activities did you see yourself engaged in?
- What colleagues or loved ones were with you?
- What was the major creative breakthrough or innovation you had?
- What was your mood?
- What did you learn from this exercise and how will it impact your life?

MANAGERS MANAGE MEETINGS

I often hear clients complaining that they have too many work meetings in their life, but they don't stop to reflect on the purpose of those meetings. If you are unhappy or dissatisfied with the pace of your life, and specifically with the plethora of meetings you attend, think outside the conference room. Are all the meetings necessary? Do all participants have to be at every meeting? Is there another way to meet (at least some of the time)? What strategy serves the needs of the project or your team best? Perhaps in addition to limiting the number of meetings, you can think how to change your role in these meetings so they are more satisfying to you and more productive in general. Being on a high-performing, collegial team can be one of the most efficient and enjoyable ways of doing less and accomplishing more.

Managing projects is a lot about meetings. To make these meetings as efficient and enjoyable as possible, first answer a few probing questions. Let your intuition unfold, and be as specific and precise as possible:

- What is your vision of success about the specific project? State it simply and clearly, in a way that conveys an aspect of larger, perhaps noble purpose; to do so is energizing to all participants, including you.

- What are the specific next steps toward success, and who can be the key players to help you accomplish this goal?

- Is yours already a shared vision or will you need to build consensus? If people envision the project differently, how will you build consensus so all participants give their best effort and bring their particular skills to the project?

- What problem(s) are you trying to solve? Does your vision directly address these problems?

- What will success look like in the next three weeks, three months, year, three to five years?

The Distractions Quotient

As a manager, on a regular basis, check to see how you are doing in terms of the plan you have set out for yourself or for your team. Depending on the project and the situation, this might mean stopping and assessing several times daily, weekly, monthly, or quarterly. Develop ways to measure the results of your actions. Regularly check to see if you are meeting, exceeding, or falling short of your plan, as well as to see how you and your team feel about your work. Be honest if your team feels you are spinning your wheels or if team dynamics become too fractious. Informally (or formally) track the distractions quotient: the potential for distractions is almost always there, and sometimes it can skyrocket. For instance, at the end of a day or week, rate yourself or your team, with 1 meaning "very distracted" and 10 meaning "very focused." If you consistently poll low numbers, consider making midcourse corrections to keep things from going haywire or to improve your focus and your enjoyment of the process and the project.

WORK LIKE A GREAT ATHLETE

One strategy common to most great athletes, in any sport, is to work in bursts of peak activity and then take mini-breaks. For example, one day on television I watched Shahar Peer, an Israeli who is one of the highest-ranked female tennis players in the world, play an intense and hard-fought match in the U.S. Open. In between points Shahar often turned away from the court and her opponent and closed her eyes. The commentators suggested that she was employing a visualization technique — seeing herself serving the ball into her opponent's court, or receiving the serve from her opponent and hitting the ball with speed and accuracy. Whatever she was imagining, though, she was using this time to quiet her mind, relax, and ready herself for the next point. She was taking a quick break to refocus, and it was effective.

In a 2001 *Harvard Business Review* article, "The Making of a Corporate Athlete," Jim Lohr and Tony Schwartz describe how great tennis players use rituals in between points that can lower their heart rates by 15 to 20 percent. These rituals include concentrating on their racquet strings or visualizing the next point. Lohr and Schwartz, whose consulting practice includes training athletes and training business leaders, find that "disciplines in the daily lives of people, including regular exercise and routines of shutting down throughout the day, resulted in executives working fewer hours and getting more done." Later in the article they make a somewhat arresting assertion: "[T]he real enemy of high performance is not stress, which paradoxical as it may seem, is actually the stimulus for growth. Rather, the problem is the absence of disciplined, intermittent recovery. Chronic stress without recovery depletes energy reserves, leads to burnout and breakdown, and ultimately undermines performance."

It's striking that they conclude that stress not only is not the problem but has a positive impact. To work better, we don't need to eliminate stress from our lives. This is good, because we can't. What we need to do is find ways to regulate stressful conditions and situations. For most of us, our daily lives are not so different from the flow and pace of a tennis match. As our day moves from home to work and back, we enter various "courts" full of intense and constant activity, but for only limited times. We then play games or interact with others (we may not have opponents, per se); these matches operate within a fair amount of mutually understood structure and rules, but they also include various levels of unpredictability and surprise. We constantly "serve" and "receive," not tennis balls, but words or ideas.

As in tennis, most of us have times when we work with intensity and we also have moments when we can take breaks, right in the midst of our work. I make a point to do this regularly throughout my day. As I was writing this book, I would block out periods of time, such as three hours, when I committed to just writing. This meant that during this three-hour time, I wouldn't read the newspaper, answer emails, answer the telephone, or watch tennis on television. I did, however, find it useful to stop about every twenty to thirty minutes. I stood up, relaxed, took a deep breath, and let go of what I was doing. These breaks allowed me to work with more intensity and with more freshness. These respites are the good distractions I spoke of earlier, and they can be quite renewing.

Stress Breaks

Create this same routine for yourself. While at work or while engaged in any intense activity, stop at regular intervals; take a deep breath, and let your entire body relax. If you are sitting down, stand up. Take a few small and relaxed steps. If you work standing up, sit down. Let your eyes partially close as you become aware of your breath and body. Let the muscles in your body relax. For one conscious minute, or the length of several slow breaths, let go of thinking about work or whatever problem you are engaged in — put your attention on your breath and body. Your breath is always there, and it is always a tool for stress reduction.

Develop routines and rituals for relaxing right in the midst of intense work, as well as in between bursts of work. If you are feeling intense stress in the form of anger or anxiety, stop: pause, feel your connection to the earth by noticing your feet coming into contact with the floor. This simple connection with the earth can help you to relax and to open yourself to new possibilities with more clarity and skill.

THE SECRET OF HAPPINESS: ROUTINES

Routines are human nature.
Why not create some that will mint Gold?

— Hafiz, fourteenth-century Persian poet

Someone once asked His Holiness the Dalai Lama, "If you only had one word to describe the secret of happiness, and of living a fulfilling and meaningful life, what would that word be?" Without hesitating the Dalai Lama replied, "Routines."

A routine is something that we do regularly, without questioning or planning. Once established, routines require little effort, tracking, or decision making; by definition they become a consistent part of our lives. Routines are ways of doing that don't require much conscious "doing." This is what makes routines such powerful levers for supporting behaviors, whether positive or negative.

As with distractions, our routines can help us or impede us, increase our focus and effectiveness or increase our distractedness. The best routines include those positive distractions we've already discussed — meditation, mindfulness, stress breaks, and so on. Positive routines also include all the other things we can do to balance our lives: exercising to refresh our bodies, talking with those we love, reading, going on retreats. These are activities that refresh and energize.

Positive routines are built to *exclude* severe distractions — the overstimulation and overexertion, without respite or relief, that can lead to anxiety, sleeplessness, depression, and a real lack of focus.

Why is this? Why would the Dalai Lama answer "routines" as an essential element on the path toward happiness and meaning? In what way do routines reduce "drag" and "resistance" and create ease, meaning, and a deeper sense of accomplishment?

Several answers come to mind, some of which we will examine in more depth:

- We all have routines; why not create positive ones?
- Routines are the way of nature (and we are part of nature ...).
- Routines connect us to something larger than ourselves.
- Paradoxically, through the structures provided by routines, we can develop flexibility because our minds are so much clearer and our bodies more refreshed.
- Routines can support personal growth and the transformation of old, unwanted patterns.

We All Have Routines, So Make Positive Ones

We all have routines, so why not have positive ones? Do you brush your teeth each morning and evening? Do you bathe or shower; prepare regular meals? Do you read or meditate every day, once a week, or not at all? Do you exercise three days a week, five days a week, or no days per week? Do you eat healthful or unhealthful food? Do you get up at the same time each morning, watch the same television shows, use many of the same phrases and expressions?

Since there is no avoiding routines, why not create routines that are supportive and healthy and lead toward what you want to accomplish in your life? Routines are the ways in which we take care of ourselves. Here are the three basic routines that I prescribe to nearly all of my coaching clients.

PRACTICE MEDITATION DAILY, IF POSSIBLE

As you've probably figured out by now, I often suggest that people spend fifteen to thirty minutes at the beginning of each day meditating — just sitting, just being alive, just being with your breath. This is a basic "sharpening the saw" activity, in which you are the saw. Meditation practice is a way to slow down, look deeply, and reveal ourselves to ourselves.

EXERCISE THREE DAYS PER WEEK

Regular exercise is essential to maintaining our health and taking care of our bodies and minds. By exercise, I mean getting a good solid aerobic workout for at least thirty minutes — such as by walking, running, or using an exercise machine at the gym. I recognize that not everyone can exercise in this way, but within your physical abilities, you can still make exercise part of your routine.

WRITE EVERY DAY IN A JOURNAL

Writing seems to access a different part of our brains than thinking or speaking. We can learn and grow by developing a regular writing practice. Each morning, or each night before you go to sleep, spend ten to fifteen minutes recording your thoughts, plans, fears, highlights of the day, or aspirations. Experiment with just writing without editing. Doing so is both cathartic and revealing. See if you can approach writing as an exploration, without quite knowing what you will find. Journaling helps build self-awareness by highlighting recurring problems and negative patterns that otherwise may continue without our noticing. After a week or month, go back and read what you've journaled. Do you see patterns or insights that surprise or disappoint you, or make you feel better about yourself?

Or, if journal writing is not your thing, experiment with creating a comparable routine of talking to your spouse or partner or a friend each day or each week about your thoughts, fears, current activities, and so on. These conversations can be either face-to-face or on the phone, and they should focus explicitly and intentionally on examining patterns and seeking insights; it's not just casually having chats with people.

Routines Are the Way of Nature

Our hearts pump to a rhythm, as do our lungs and all of the systems within our bodies. The sun and the moon and the oceans move and shift in cycles and patterns. Almost everything in the universe exhibits regularity. Ancient humans woke with daylight and went to sleep with darkness. Women's menstrual cycles were in tune with the cycle of the moon. Daily rhythms hold us and allow us to feel safe, creating space for play and creativity. In everything we do, we rely on and are comforted by routines.

Routines can connect us to something larger than ourselves and our preferences, to the larger web of our community and to nature and existence itself. For example, birthdays, Thanksgiving Day, New Year's, and all the other social and cultural holidays we celebrate form part of the routine of our society, one that is outside of our decision making. These and all routines can take us out of our moods by establishing patterns that are larger than the daily or hourly oscillations or inclinations of our likes and dislikes.

Routines can connect us to something larger than ourselves and our preferences, to the larger web of our community and to nature and existence itself.

Through Form, Flexibility

Zen practice describes the use of ritual and forms as "strict form/flexible mind." This expression points to the paradox that forms and routines can actually help us develop more flexible and responsive minds. Though seemingly rigid, strict routines and habits actually free us to experience our own unique presence within them; they work to our advantage mentally, physically, and spiritually.

One of my coaching clients called recently to tell me that he would be a little late for our 8 AM appointment. He said that on

Thursday mornings he goes to his synagogue to attend the morning service, and once a month he has a role reading from the Torah. When he arrived at my home office later, he was both relaxed and animated. He described the importance of this morning routine and how it added texture and meaning to the rest of his day.

I understand, since one of the richest periods of my life was when I followed a Zen monastic schedule at Tassajara Zen Mountain Center. When I lived there, each year there were two ninety-day practice periods. Each practice period had an opening ceremony and a closing ceremony. Every calendar day that contained a four or a nine (the fourth, ninth, fourteen, nineteenth, and so on) was a day off. On these days we "slept in" until 5 AM, instead of rising with the usual 3:30 AM wake-up bell. Every day that contained a three or an eight (third, eighth, thirteenth, and so on) was called "the day before day off." On these days there was a somewhat different schedule and a ritual to prepare for day off. Then, every day, there were routines for the serving and eating of meals, routines for meditation practice, routines for studying, and even routines for taking a bath and using the toilet.

The reason these disciplined monastic months felt so enriching to me was that I was required to follow a demanding yet doable schedule. Living a life filled with routines was such a relief. Routines provided a container and structure to activity that was surprisingly freeing. At the same time, that set of routines allowed me to see all sorts of paths of resistance more clearly.

Mint Gold

Routines are already an integral part of your life. Examine them closely and with some sense of generosity toward yourself. You may as well form routines that will mint gold.

One way to start is to make a list of the routines you currently have in your day, especially in the morning: showering or bathing; brushing your teeth; shaving or putting on makeup; preparing and enjoying your first cup of coffee; making breakfast for your family; dressing your children; exercise, such as walking, stretching, or yoga; checking email first thing in the morning; listening to voicemails that accumulated overnight; text messaging; participating in predawn conference calls (people do this!); sleeping till the last minute and dashing off to work without any personal time; your commute, whether you're driving, carpooling, or taking public transportation; and so on. Then identify what routines you would like to drop, as well as some possible routines to add in the context of what would support your ability to accomplish more with less effort.

Above all, enjoy this process of taking a personal inventory and re-creating your routines so your life is more functional and replenishing. The almost tidal aspects of daily life really can be wonderful and are available to all of us.

INSATIABLE WANTS

The subject of being overly busy, the impact of information technology on our work lives and our souls, and the use of meditative practices as antidotes to crazy-busyness have been passions of mine for many years. An expert in these congruent fields is David Levy, a professor of information technology at the University of Washington in Seattle. His particular area of study is the relationship between technology, information overload, and contemplative practices. In his groundbreaking paper "No Time to Think," he describes some of the historical events that have contributed to our current more-faster-better mindset. Going back nearly one hundred years, in the late 1920s the U.S. government was concerned that the country had reached the peak of the Industrial Revolution. A major study was undertaken to see if the development of new products — and even the desire for them — was waning. Here Professor Levy comments on the study's findings:

> The 1929 report of Herbert Hoover's Committee on Recent Economic Changes captured the tone of gleeful discovery: "The survey has proved conclusively what has long been held theoretically to be true, that wants are almost insatiable; that one want satisfied makes way endlessly for newer wants, as fast as they are satisfied...." Viewed in this historical light, today's concerns about busyness, about the accelerating pace of life, and about the surfeit of information and the difficulty of managing it are a fairly straightforward extrapolation of past trends — the latest manifestation of a "more-faster-better" philosophy of life.

Underneath these "insatiable wants" is the fact that we are making choices each moment of each day. We choose to live a particular lifestyle, we choose if and when to check emails, to accomplish certain goals, to drive to work. It can be difficult, sometimes nearly impossible, to distinguish between what we really need, what we want, and what is a distraction. There are no fixed rules for determining these.

The practices presented in this chapter are ways to increase your awareness and support your ability to make choices — choices that allow you to move into your authenticity and real power so that you can accomplish today that which you most hope to achieve in the larger context of your life. In this regard, work and career, title and promotions, matter a lot because they offer goalposts and a sense of movement and progress. But ultimately, "success" in our work world and in our life does not rest with external rewards or achievements. What matters most is how much love and goodness our existence has added to the planet, how effectively we have engaged with the people we cherish most, and how much we have been able to locate our own sense of deep composure right in the midst of the messiness of life.

RESISTANCE

Have patience with everything unresolved in your heart
And try to love the questions themselves.

— Rilke

ON THE SUBJECT OF CHANGE, the Buddhists got it right. Everything changes. Everything is impermanent. Everything that we
take for granted is changing, constantly. The formation of the
clouds in the sky at this moment is unique and will never be
repeated. Every cell in our bodies is replaced, some quickly, some
more slowly, every seven years. Our planet and the universe are
in a state of continual, inconceivable transformation. As I write,
the price of gasoline has skyrocketed to over four dollars per gal-
lon. By the time you read this book, this price may seem outrageously inexpensive or very high.

The fact that everything changes is good news. Or, actually, as
the Buddhists and scientists would say, it is neither good news nor
bad news. It is what is, neither good nor bad...and this is good

news! However, we often find it difficult to accept change and the uncertainty that goes along with it. We grasp at what we know and what is familiar and resist anything that might change them. Our desires can also be a form of resistance: perhaps we want things to be different than they are, or we desire a particular outcome, a certain future, and we resist other possibilities. When we stop resisting what is or what might be, when we let go of grasping at what we have or what we want, we see that change is neither good nor bad. When we do this, we can see our lives and the world the way they actually are. We become more effective because we can respond appropriately to any situation. Like change, no event is ever wholly bad or wholly good. For example, a negative effect of expensive gasoline is that it puts an undue burden on those with lower incomes, since high gas prices drive up the costs for everyday necessities, such as food, clothes, and household items. On the other hand, a positive effect of higher gas prices is that they will encourage the development of alternative energy sources and better forms of public transportation, resulting in fewer greenhouse gasses and a less gasoline-dependent world.

We inhabit a changing, dynamic world in continual flux. When we don't cling to what we have and resist change, we can more fully enter the situation at hand and be more open to learning from whatever may arise. As with all the aspects of the Less Manifesto, this is easier to see and understand than it is to implement in our daily lives.

MAN OVERBOARD!

Last summer I went on a two-day river rafting trip on the Kern River in southern California with my teenage daughter as the river guide. I was proud to see my baby girl (then nineteen years old) skillfully and confidently maneuvering our inflatable raft through a variety of challenging white-water conditions. I also found it humbling to have my daughter giving commands and barking orders as to when and how to paddle.

As we approached the largest rapid on the river I could feel my heart beating faster. Upon entering the turbulent water, our boat got stuck on a large boulder. I was in the front of the boat and reached forward with my paddle, thinking I would help push us away from the rock. In the next instant I could feel myself falling out of the boat and into the river. What a feeling: "Oh, I'm falling out of the boat." I was surprised, and I must admit, I did have my moments of resistance (and terror). "Why me, how could I be so stupid? I cannot really be falling out of the boat!"

This resistance evaporated quickly, as I landed in the cold, powerfully churning water. Despite my high-quality flotation vest, I was pulled underwater, but thankfully, within seconds I popped back up to the surface. It was quite exhilarating, even though also terrifying. A few moments later one of the other trip leaders called for me to float toward his boat, where I was quickly pulled up and in. I was shaken, out of breath, and quite relieved to be out of the churning water.

An equivalent of this experience happens all the time in our lives — we are cut off by another driver on the road; our child is suddenly hurt and crying; our boss enters our office and announces an impromptu meeting for which we know we are not prepared; we receive an aggressive and attacking email; our flight is delayed; someone we love becomes gravely ill or is faced with a crisis. This is life. You cannot count on things going smoothly. When we do, we often wind up sorely disappointed and unhappy. Resisting change, which often arrives suddenly and unexpectedly, keeps us from seeing the scenario unfolding before us clearly, and it can keep us from acting in ways that are effective and nimble and that lead to results that make us feel good and proud of ourselves. Here are a variety of strategies for reducing resistance to change and increasing your personal and professional effectiveness.

THE POWER OF POSITIVE PRIMING

[M]uch of the time, we are simply operating on automatic pilot,
and the way we think and act and how well we think and act
on the spur of the moment, are a lot more susceptible
to outside influences than we realize.

— Malcolm Gladwell, *Blink*

John A. Bargh and Tanya L. Chartrand in *The Unbearable Automaticity of Being* described an experiment they conducted in which two groups of students were given the same series of math and financial problems to solve. In the room with one group, a briefcase was placed on the table. In the room with the other group, a backpack was placed on the table. The group with the briefcase achieved significantly higher test scores than the group with the backpack. The briefcase, which conjures images of business and competition, "primes" people to be more focused and competitive than does a backpack, which primes people for relaxed walking and hiking. "Priming" is a psychological term that refers to representations or associations in memory that influence behavior. Priming prepares or sensitizes the person being primed. For example, if, after having been primed by reading the word "computer," you are later asked to complete a word beginning with "com," you are more likely to answer "computer." We can all use priming to make positive associations, which, as the students demonstrated, can lead to more effective results.

Recently, a coaching client of mine, who is a very successful entrepreneur and visionary, was describing her next day's schedule to me: "I have an 8 AM breakfast meeting, followed by a 9 AM meeting on the other side of town. Then I have a conference call at 9:45 and a 10:30 meeting back at my office. I will have a really impossible day tomorrow."

I stopped her right away. "So, you plan to have an impossible day? Have you thought about this? Is this really what you want? How does it make you feel? What about planning on having a different kind of day? What different kind of scheduling might be possible?"

"OK," she laughed. "I'll at least reschedule my 9 AM meeting, and see if there's some flexibility about when the conference call has to begin. Yes, I will plan to have an engaging and perhaps even relaxing day."

The next time you anticipate a meeting at work, notice what your beliefs are about yourself and about how the meeting will go. If either or both are negative, can you reconceive them in a positive way? Any time we approach a task, we should stop, take our mental pulse, and make sure our attitude and expectations are positive. If the presence of a backpack can influence someone's ability to solve math problems, how much more powerful is your attitude and what you imagine the outcome of a situation will be? For the next week, before you initiate a conversation, undertake a task, or enter a meeting, pay attention to your underlying attitudes about it. Often our worries, concerns, and doubts contribute to beliefs that block our creativity or enjoyment of the process. Like the backpack, they may be inadvertently undermining the outcome we most deeply want.

Often our worries, concerns, and doubts contribute to beliefs that block our creativity or enjoyment of the process.

Ovid, a Roman poet who lived more than two thousand years ago, told the story of a sculptor, Pygmalion, who created a statue of the ideal woman. The result was so beautiful that Pygmalion fell desperately in love with his own creation. Pygmalion prayed to the gods, asking them to make the sculpture real. His statue came to life and, as the story goes, the couple lived happily ever after.

Today, the *Pygmalion effect* is the name given to this dynamic of how our beliefs influence outcomes. For example, educational researchers Robert Rosenthal and Lenore Jacobson, in their book *Pygmalion in the Classroom*, show that a classroom teacher's belief about the potential or lack of potential of a student has a profound influence on the performance of that student. Thus, what we believe, or what we are primed to believe by others or our environment, can become a self-fulfilling prophecy.

The Pygmalion effect is often invoked in a negative sense, as a way beliefs can limit or control us, but the underlying dynamic is neither positive nor negative. What we believe influences the outcome. These beliefs can be brought into awareness, and if necessary they can be reframed so that they support our efforts. Since we are constantly being primed, why not use this dynamic toward achieving positive outcomes?

Often we hold on to limiting and self-defeating beliefs because it seems safer; these ideas reflect what we think we know about ourselves or the world (I'm not a good cook; I don't speak well in public). Sometimes we resist even positive change rather than let go of what we already have. What we have seems comfortable, even when in truth the results are pretty *un*comfortable.

Here are some ways to experiment with more open-ended beliefs. Exploring how your beliefs can be transformed can alter your thinking and actions. It may also reduce your overall resistance. Below is a list I recently formulated for myself. Compile your own list of limiting beliefs and rephrase them as open-ended beliefs, using what I have included here as a guide. Then write down your open-ended beliefs on sticky notes or three-by-five index cards as daily reminders placed in your office, wallet, or purse. Notice how, one at a time, these more open-ended beliefs challenge your more limiting beliefs. Also, consider what you gain from holding on to your limiting beliefs. There are always reasons — often fairly compelling though not particularly useful ones — that we hold on to limiting beliefs for so long.

COMMON LIMITING BELIEFS	MORE OPEN-ENDED BELIEFS
I don't have time (I'm too busy!).	I am clear about priorities and my ability to respond.
I don't have enough experience.	I know my strengths and what I still need to learn.
I'm not smart enough.	I love to learn new things and I'm smart enough.
I'm not worthy enough.	I am more effective than I think I am.
I'm usually quite stubborn.	I can learn from my mistakes.
I don't have the resources.	I know how to enroll and enlist others and gather resources.

Self-limiting beliefs get in the way much more than we might imagine. Looking at and owning these beliefs can sometimes be embarrassing. Unearthing and becoming aware of our limiting beliefs is not easy, and it is a process that we may never fully complete. As we step beyond and resolve our current negative beliefs and fears, new and perhaps more deeply held beliefs may arise for us to contend with.

Practice Emotional Change

Toward the end of his book *Working with Emotional Intelligence*, Daniel Goleman titles one chapter "The Billion Dollar Mistake." In it he describes how emotional change requires more than intellectual understanding. Organizations that introduce programs for developing emotional change and then teach its principles as though teaching computer science usually find that the results are sorely lacking. Emotional change requires practice and repetition. Grasping for what is known and seemingly safe, even when it holds you back or undermines you, is a difficult behavior to change. This underscores the need to experiment regularly with several practices — such as daily meditation, openly receiving feedback, learning to be a better listener, and creating positive routines in your life.

Here is another one to try:

Make a list of what you think of as your limiting beliefs. Just write them down, notice them, bring them into awareness.

Then ask yourself: Are these beliefs true?

Why do I think they are true?

What if they were not true?

PRECISE OBSERVATIONS

A coaching client of mine is the CEO of a fast-growing media company. In one of our initial meetings, he mentioned his money challenges, and I asked to see his cash-flow projections. I was rather surprised when he told me he didn't have any. How, then, did he track and project his cash needs? He said his way of tracking cash flow was "by feeling and gauging the amount of pain and tightness in my chest."

As he said this, I realized that this is how we often generalize problems and difficult situations. We know something is painful —

something is out of alignment in our personal lives or out of whack in our business transactions — yet we don't take the next step of looking more closely or deeply at the situation and at what is needed to fix or improve it. In this sense, avoidance becomes a way of resisting; it's a way to hold on to what is familiar and comfortable — even when doing so causes emotional and physical pain.

My client and I immediately sat down at his computer, and for the next two hours we gathered his financial records, created a spreadsheet showing his cash position, and produced a first draft of a three-month cash-flow projection. Though his business condition was not rosy, since he had some immediate cash-flow challenges, having a clear picture of his financial status and a projection of the future helped ease his chest pain. He now could take practical and effective action — he knew what bills he could pay, what customers owed him money, what the remainder of the quarter looked like financially. This cash-flow projection opened up a world of possibilities and options for his immediate and long-term choices as well as for crafting a smarter business. Reliable information had replaced vague fears.

The clearer you are about your *actual* situation, the less you will grasp at your *ideas* or fears regarding your current situation. This opens up possibilities for innovation and transformation. A business plan is a reality check. You may be reluctant to let go of or change your vision and goals, but isn't it better to adjust your flight plan than to blindly crash and burn

> The clearer you are about your *actual* situation, the less you will grasp at your *ideas* or fears regarding your current situation.

because you were afraid to look at your fuel gauge or a map? If you want to accomplish more, it's important to identify what, to quantify your vision. Measurements and timelines help track our progress, and they also help identify what gets in the way of realizing our plans. Similarly, if you want to do less, to simplify your life, be precise about how. You may long to feel less busy, but to achieve this you need to translate it into specifics: What are your benchmarks, timelines, and measurements for downsizing your workload or adjusting your schedule? What other adjustments or healthy activities will support your goal of feeling less hurried? Where, precisely, do you need to make changes?

Observing Precisely and Creating Systems

We can increase our observational skills through practice. Here is a list of activities to try:

- Almost like a meditation, pay attention to what is right in front of you — what do you see, hear, smell, taste, and touch? For at least five minutes, try to take in every tiny aspect of your physical environment.
- Think about what energizes you and what drains you. Are there links between your energy, your activity, and your feelings? If you're so inclined, create diagrams or flow-charts that show these relationships. Though this may seem paradoxical with emotions, try surrendering to the details, to the practice of precision.
- Track your money flow and your overall financial condition — in your business and at home. Create a system or routine to track work and personal financial projections.

I suggest that your systems generally be straightforward, repeatable, and enjoyable. For me, the last day of each month is a signal to assess my actual revenue against my projected revenue. The last day of each quarter is a signal to check how my business performance has compared to my vision and strategy. The more you know about the facts of your work life and home life, the more relaxed your mind, and the greater the possibility of creativity as well as peace of mind.

A last word about creating systems. My idea of a terrific system is this: I place the folders that I need for the day on top of my shoes by the front door of my home. This, I believe, is an example of intelligent simplicity — it's a clearly simple and nearly foolproof system designed to overcome any forgetfulness or lack of intelligence on my part. Of course, any system of reminders and organization that works for you and is effective is fine. But typically, the easier the system is to maintain, and the more obvious the reminders, the more successful it will be.

INTEGRATIVE THINKING

According to Roger Martin, dean of the University of Toronto Business School, focusing on what a successful leader *does* is a mistake. Martin contends that it's more beneficial to study how great leaders *think*. In his studies of successful leaders, he has concluded that they process information differently than the rest of us do.

In *How Successful Leaders Think*, Martin writes that successful leaders "have the predisposition and the capacity to hold in their head two opposing ideas at once. And then, without panicking or simply settling for one alternative or the other, they're able to creatively resolve the tension between those two ideas by generating a new one that contains elements of the others but is superior to both."

Martin calls this process of consideration and synthesis "integrative thinking," and he contends that it is this ability and not a "superior strategy or faultless execution that is the defining characteristic of most exceptional businesses and the people who run them." Martin interviewed fifty exemplary leaders in doing his research, and, intriguingly, he says that many successful executives aren't even aware that this is the way they go about processing information.

We are continually faced with having to make choices — from what business strategies to pursue to how to approach career and relationships. We also face an enormous array of more mundane choices, large and small. Many times, we face simple either/or situations, in which we must choose one thing or another — whether to purchase a half or a full pint of blueberries, whether we want paper or plastic bags, whether to drive to our next appointment or take a bus. Most choices, though, are not as clear-cut.

For example, in my current coaching and consulting company, I have no employees on the payroll. I like this freedom, especially after fifteen years as a CEO. However, if I want to grow ZBA Associates, I have to decide in what direction and how to handle the increased workload. Should I emphasize personal coaching or corporate consulting, or pursue both? Should I hire (and train) other coaches to do what I do, or should I hire marketing and financial people to take those tasks away from me so I can coach more and write more? Should these people be employees, or should I contract these services out? I am faced with a variety of options, and I need to make choices, and in some cases, I may start to feel stuck because none of my choices seem appealing, or they may seem to cancel each other out.

In these cases I can utilize the methodology and practice of integrative thinking — rather than remaining stuck in an either/or dilemma, feeling that I must walk down one of two divergent paths, I can reimagine the problem, or combine the best of both solutions, in order to create a new and better path.

In another example, a few years ago my then-seventeen-year-old daughter announced that she wanted to spend six months living in a remote village in western Africa. To my wife and I, this didn't seem like a good idea. At first, all three of us could think only in terms of yes or no. Could she go or not? Eventually, my wife and I realized that we wanted to support our daughter's passion and courage, but we needed to devise a situation in which we felt that she would be safe, or at least as safe as we could realistically plan for. So we set to work to create that scenario — which in part involved having someone whom we could trust be responsible for looking after her safety in Africa and having our daughter agree to check in with us via telephone once a week. Once we got beyond yes/no thinking, we all got what we wanted by crafting an amalgam of solutions.

Much of our lives involves integrative thinking. It was while managing a Zen monastery that I observed that business and spirituality were not at odds with each other. I did not have to choose between the everyday world and the sacred or spiritual. In my Accomplishing More by Doing Less workshops I've begun to use practices from the world of improvisational theater to develop leadership skills and build self-awareness.

Try bringing integrative awareness to a problem you face: Make a list of some of the key dilemmas that you face right now at work or in your home life. Choose one (or several, considered one at a time): on a sheet of paper, list the pros and cons of each choice you see for solving the dilemma. Make sure that for each pro or con item you clearly state the reason that it is a pro or a con. Now compare those lists of pros and cons. Where exactly do the choices conflict, and where do they not? Is there a potential amalgam of the best pros with the least troublesome cons? Next, see if you can craft a series of if/then statements that describe the conditions for which certain unavoidable cons would be acceptable. In the example with my daughter, we essentially said, if we can be assured of your reasonable safety, then we'll approve the trip. This showed us a way to get past the binary dilemma of an either/or solution. As you do your comparison, do you notice any particular beliefs or emotions that block all options; are you resisting change itself, or grasping at old, comforting habits even if they're in your way? If so, step back from the particular dilemma and see how you might resolve the emotion first. With integrative thinking, we are always challenged to look beyond our comfort zone, beyond what we already know, to see new and unfamiliar solutions and paths.

INSPIRING CREATIVITY

The less we cling to what we know, the more open we are to creativity. Conversely, the more creative we train ourselves to be, the less resistant to change we'll be.

Jules-Henri Poincaré, a nineteenth-century mathematician, defined a four-step process for creativity. 1) Preparation: define the problem, understand what has already been tried, and take whatever actions are required to embark on the creative process. 2) Incubation: reflect and daydream; let the issue or problem take root in your psyche and in your life. 3) Illumination: the "aha" moment of discovery, in which a new idea or new way of doing something arises. 4) Execution: put the creative discovery into action, which often requires a good deal of persistence and trial and error.

In our intensely busy, high-pressured world, we often want to go directly to step three, the aha moment, without spending time in the preparation or incubation phase. Then it is all too common to underestimate the importance of execution, which not only requires persistence and patience but generally requires enlisting the help and expertise of others.

In addition to the four steps outlined by the mathematician

Poincaré, creativity is also aided and inspired by four important approaches suggested by Michael Ray, a former Stanford Graduate Business School professor. He developed and taught one of the all-time most popular graduate business courses at Stanford. Here are his four approaches:

1.   Trust in your own creativity: Have confidence in your creative abilities. If you lack confidence, begin by naming three of the most creative things you've initiated or taken part in. How does being creative feel? Are there ways you have been and are creative that are nontypical? Perhaps you enjoy baking, or karaoke, or crafting your own photo albums. Encourage your creativity by drawing, writing poetry, or journaling.

2.   Be less self-judging: Everyone I've ever known has an inner judge. But I have also noticed that nearly everyone believes that the voice of his or her inner judge is louder and more persistent than anyone else's. It can be difficult to accept that having an inner critic is part of the human condition. Knowing this, experiment with relaxing and giving yourself a break. Despite your judgments, you do have the ability to be creative. Everyone does.

     Pay attention to your judging voice. Become friends with it. Instead of trying to push it away, invite it in and play with it. The more you push away your inner critic, the louder and more persistent it can become. If you relax, listen, and learn from this voice, it may become quieter and at times silent.

3.   Pay attention to details. Through the creative process, we see the things around us in new ways that most people may not. Pay attention to what is most obvious, to what is right in front of you.

One fun experiment is to give objects new names. For instance, take a paper clip. Examine it closely, like you just invented it — what might you call it? Try this with a telephone, a T-shirt, a strawberry, or any other everyday object in your life. Often we take familiar objects for granted and fail to notice their exquisite form and detail. Giving them new names is a way to see them with fresh eyes.

4. There are no dumb questions: Our desire to look good or smart can get in the way of creativity. Instead, question everything. Risk looking awkward. Make it a practice to look underneath the surface of things, to question why you do things the way you do.

I'm reminded of a question that my then-nineteen-year-old son asked while we were driving several years ago, when I was still CEO of Brush Dance. He held up a spiritual golf calendar that Brush Dance had recently published and asked in a challenging tone, "Why did you publish this calendar? What were you thinking? How many people would buy a calendar about spiritual golf?" At first I was taken aback by my son's questioning, his dismissive tone, and his doubting of decisions I had made. I acknowledged that this calendar had not been very successful, and I realized he was actually raising an important question that deserved to be asked — How do we make our decisions about what calendars to produce? My son then blurted out that he could, in about five minutes, think of an idea for a calendar title that was better than anything we had ever done. I turned to him and said, "Okay, you've got five minutes. Go." He closed his eyes and sat quietly, obviously thinking. Then, a few minutes later, he opened his eyes and said, "I've got it. You should create a calendar with images of people's smiles." I had to admit, this was a terrific idea.

KAIZEN: SMALL CHANGES FOR BIG RESULTS

Many times, we resist change because change seems too big. Change is easier to accept, and to practice, when it's small. This is the secret power of Kaizen.

Originally a Japanese management concept designed to improve business practices, Kaizen is a process aimed at reducing or eliminating unnecessary physical and mental work. It encourages people to create and perform experiments as part of their daily work lives in order to become aware of and eliminate waste in their jobs. The ultimate goal of Kaizen is to accomplish more by doing less.

In the book *Gemba Kaizen*, Masaaki Imai quotes Edward C. Johnson III, chairman and CEO of Fidelity Investments: "Kaizen — the spirit that whatever you're doing, you can do better — gave us the foundation we needed to work as a team in setting and reaching higher service standards. It also helped us successfully weather a rough patch in our investment business.... Over the years, we've seen many strategies for management success come and go. In my experience, Kaizen is different. It's not a fad. It helps us focus in a very basic way on how we do our work. The process of doing our work becomes an end in itself as well as a means of gratification. For me, that's where the real joy comes in."

A business associate of mine recently had lunch with an executive from Fidelity Investments. The Fidelity executive shared with my friend that Fidelity has more than forty thousand employees and that the term "Kaizen," though not written down anywhere in the company's materials, is on the lips of all forty thousand employees.

Then, just by coincidence, a few days after this I met with a local Fidelity representative. Within the first few minutes of our conversation, the representative mentioned the practice of Kaizen. He said that at their weekly staff meetings, each person was expected to address how they had implemented Kaizen in their work — each person was expected to identify one small improvement they had made or planned to make in the coming week. This sounded to me like a practical and effective method of enjoying the process of change, rather than resisting and grasping at what is known and comfortable.

Reduce your own resistance to change and practice Kaizen in your own life. Ask yourself: What is one change I could make in my life today that would have an impact on the quality of my day?

Ask yourself: What is one change you could make in your life today that would have an impact on the quality of your day?

Everything is constantly changing — your body, your intentions, your life, the environment — and this simple practice lets you gently enter and dance in the stream of change.

Take a moment to reflect, and write down your answer to the question — identify one change in your life. This change doesn't need to be large — just one small, even seemingly insignificant difference. This change could be in the way you do something, it could be something you stop doing, or it could be a small adjustment of your outlook or attitude. By focusing on one item, giving it your attention, and measuring it, you can reduce resistance and increase your effectiveness.

Traditional Kaizen practice is generally guided by three core principles:

1. RESULTS: Create benchmarks and measurements for a process in your work, or for a particular project. Create a way to quantify the impact of the change.
2. SYSTEMIC THINKING: Pay attention to the larger picture. How does what you do fit into the overall system? Who connects with what you do? How can these systems and relationships be measured and improved?

3. A NONJUDGMENTAL, NONBLAMING ATTITUDE: This is an important part of the Kaizen practice. Not only do judgment and blaming interfere with making improvements, but judgment and blaming are by themselves unnecessary and wasteful and encourage more resistance.

People at all levels of an organization can participate in Kaizen, from the CEO down. And Kaizen can be practiced in any setting: by individuals, by small or large groups, by families. Kaizen is not a competition; it operates under the principle that an individual cannot benefit at another's expense. It is also never static or finished. In Kaizen methodology, one makes changes, monitors results, and then adjusts, in a continual cycle.

Here is an overview of that cycle:

1. Pay attention to the details, especially the small ones, of your activity.
2. Create goals or benchmarks and ways to compare what you actually do to those benchmarks.
3. Create innovations and put these into action.
4. Pay attention and measure the results of these innovations.
5. Find a way to incorporate these improvements, in ways that are practical and concrete.
6. Continue this cycle.

The issues and practices introduced here remind me of a program I've been helping to develop at a cutting-edge technology company; we call it Search Inside Yourself. During the first class we explain that searching is necessary to develop self-understanding, to build emotional intelligence and leadership abilities. Some structure and intention is useful to support the process of searching. You don't know exactly what you are looking for. You let go of your conceptions, your grasping for answers, and drop down into a deeper way of looking at yourself and the world. The result can be surprisingly rewarding.

The practices in this chapter — positive priming, precise observations, integrative thinking, fostering creativity, and Kaizen — are intended to help open you to change. They are tools for increasing your personal capacity without exhausting yourself, for developing flexibility and responsiveness in terms of how you think about yourself. My hope is that as you use them you will come to think about yourself (and others) more kindly and with less judgment. What we know, the expertise we gain through experience, is useful, but clinging to what we know can also be surprisingly self-defeating. The more we resist change, the more likely we are to develop habituated, dysfunctional patterns. In ways large and small, the more we embrace change, opening ourselves and our ways of thinking to new approaches and ideas, the better equipped we will be to achieve much more of what we truly hope to achieve.

CHAPTER 8

BUSYNESS, OR FINDING THE ONE WHO IS NOT BUSY

It is not enough to be busy. So are the ants.
The question is: what are we busy about?

— Henry David Thoreau

THERE IS A STORY ABOUT TWO ZEN TEACHERS from seventh-century China. One teacher is sweeping some stone steps inside the monastery with a wooden broom. He is approached by the other teacher, who looks at him and remarks, "Too busy." (This is a way of saying, "Why are you sweeping when you should be meditating or undertaking some type of contemplative practice?") The first teacher, holding his broom, responds by saying, "You should know that there is one who is not busy."

Though we often associate busyness with activity and speed, and lack of busyness with stopping or slowing down, this is not always the case. It is possible to be actively engaged and not be busy. Not being "busy" does not require that you stop, slow down, or step out of the activity of your life. Most of the time, we learn, we adjust, we find our composure, right in the midst of the activity and intensity of our lives. We have to!

LESS EFFORT, MORE RESULTS

In *Extraordinary Golf*, Fred Shoemaker describes a study comparing the golf swings of top professional golfers with the swings of average golfers that provides some useful lessons about doing, effort, and effortlessness. The study shows three different rows of golfers, detailing their various golf swings. In the top row is a professional golfer. In the second row is an average golfer hitting a golf ball. In the third row is an average golfer swinging when there is no ball. The study found that when an average golfer is not trying to hit a golf ball, his or her swing more closely resembles the swing of a professional golfer. When an average golfer is actually hitting a golf ball, his or her swing changes for the worse.

It appears that when a golfer is not aiming for any result, the golfer can replicate the better, more professional swing. Put a ball on the tee, and the golfer tries too hard or exerts unnecessary effort, which gets in the way of the natural, effective knowledge that is resident within the mind and body.

Lack of striving by itself does not lead to an effective golf swing (nor does it make you more focused, more emotionally present, or a better leader). Being effective requires study, practice, and skill building, which at the point of performance combines with effortlessness. It's particularly significant that this study of golf swings highlights the negative impact of extra effort, of trying too hard.

I cite this study not to improve your golf game (though for some it could be a useful unintended consequence) but to offer a quantifiable example of a lesson that can be applied to anything and everything in your life. Tension, anxiety, extra effort, an overly busy mind, our inner critic, any negative inner voice: these all can interfere with a calm, composed mind and affect our performance.

In this golf study, we see a perfect illustration of the central theme of this book: less effort accomplishes more. Less striving, less trying, less racing, less pushing can lead to surprisingly better results. At the same time, the work we do becomes less exhausting, less emotionally taxing. In a very real way, when we reduce *busyness*, the productivity of our business improves — whether it's our personal business or the profit-oriented kind.

> **Less striving, less trying, less racing, less pushing can lead to surprisingly better results.**

Sitting and Walking

One way to explore "finding the one who is not busy" is to ask yourself: What am I doing that is extra? Then for a few hours during the day, pay attention to simple everyday physical activities like walking or sitting. Yes, pay attention to how you walk and how you sit down. Do you hold your shoulders tightly or are they relaxed and comfortable? Is your walking fluid and flowing or is there effort and strain in your gait? Notice where you carry tension in your muscles, and when you notice it, relax. Take a deep breath and let the tension go. Continue to do this regularly throughout the day, paying attention to your body and your posture, and reducing stress and tension. By the end of the day, do you notice any change? Do you have less tension, and when you feel it, is it easier to let it go? It can take a lot of practice and attention to relearn ingrained physical habits, but doing so has enormous benefits. Depending on how hard this is for you, and how much tension you carry, consider working with a physical trainer or engaging in another type of bodywork: yoga, Pilates, sensory awareness, and Alexander Technique are a few examples.

Now ask this same question — "What am I doing extra? Where am I holding tension?" — during other everyday activities, such as composing emails or writing at the computer screen. Are your attitude and approach relaxed? Are you thinking too hard? Can you reduce or release this extra effort? Practice doing so on a regular basis and see if your productivity, or your swing, doesn't improve.

TAKE A BREAK FOR A BREAKTHROUGH

We're all familiar with this paradox: we struggle our hardest for weeks without success to find a solution to a particularly difficult problem, and then one day, while we're stopping and thinking about nothing in particular, the answer hits us like a bolt from the blue. Why is this? One of the most famous examples of a break leading to a breakthrough happened 2,200 years ago when Archimedes, the great Greek mathematician, was taking a bath.

As the story goes, Archimedes took on the challenge of determining whether the king's gold crown had been fraudulently manufactured. While mulling over how to solve this problem, he took a trip to the public baths. While in the tub, he observed that the more his body sank into the water, the more water was displaced. He concluded that since gold weighs more than silver, a crown mixed with silver would have to be bulkier to reach the same weight as one composed only of gold, and it would therefore displace more water than its pure gold counterpart. Realizing he'd hit upon the answer to his challenge, he leaped out of the bath and rushed home naked, crying, "Eureka! Eureka!" — "I've found it! I've found it!"

Though the story is no doubt apocryphal, this same experience is repeated numerous times in our lives. We have "eureka" moments in the shower, or while walking in the forest or along the beach, or sometimes even while doing the dishes or quietly driving to work. As many psychological experiments have shown, this is because creativity is fostered when our minds are relaxed and open, which is not the case when we are actively engaged in the effort to solve a particular problem. We often experience this when waking up from sleep, the ultimate break — we see a problem completely differently than we did before sleep. This is because when we let go of our conscious mind, our unconscious mind has a chance to do some pretty amazing work.

Conscious Wandering

Mark Jung-Beeman is a cognitive neuroscientist at Northwestern University, and he has studied what happens inside the brain when people have an insight. He was quoted in a recent *New Yorker* article, saying: "If you want to encourage insights, then you've got to also encourage people to relax." The article notes that "Jung-Beeman's latest paper investigates why people who are in a good mood are so much better at solving insight puzzles."

What Jung-Beeman has discovered is that insight and creative solutions can be inhibited or blocked by our being overly focused. Instead, what is often needed for insight is to focus on not focusing. The article continues, "As Jung-Beeman and Kounios [a cognitive neuroscientist at Drexel University] see it, the insight process is an act of cognitive deliberation — the brain must be focused on the task at hand — transformed by accidental, serendipitous connections. We must concentrate, but we must concentrate on letting the mind wander."

In other words, in order to increase our ability to innovate or solve particularly difficult problems, we need to find the one who is not busy.

This notion may seem to contradict what I said in chapter 6 about the benefits of focused attention, but it doesn't. The difference is context. When we are beset by too many distractions, whether sensory or internal, we need to lessen distractions and increase our focus to be effective. However, when we become overfocused, so that our bodies and minds tense up with all the extra effort we're expending, we need to distract ourselves in a positive way. Then, we need to relax and allow our minds to wander in order to be open to the next great Aha!

It can be difficult, especially in the midst of stress and pressure, to pause and relax. It may seem counterintuitive to take breaks in order to increase our creativity and ability to accomplish more, but it is remarkably beneficial to do so. And yet, as we discussed in chapter 6, and as we experience daily, this is harder and harder in our media- and technology-saturated world. When we do take breaks, we usually fill all of our spare moments with podcasts and phone conversations, web browsing and texting, and watching TV and films. Increasingly, we carry all our entertainment and communication options in our pockets. This is now an embedded aspect of contemporary life and it offers many benefits. But would Archimedes have had his eureka moment if he'd gone to the baths and immediately started catching up on email while trolling the Internet for half-priced togas? The breaks that lead to breakthroughs must foster open-ended mental wandering; they quiet the noise and busyness in our brains and relax us physically. We must literally turn off the noise and engage in activities that are refreshingly quiet. In fact, many of the practices I discuss throughout the book can help you foster this, by creating a routine of mindfulness that you can access whenever you need it.

For many years, when I was CEO of Brush Dance, I often went for walks during my lunch hour or at the end of the day, with the intention of quieting my mind to allow for new calendar or greeting card ideas to arise. When I worked with artists in developing new ideas, we would often begin our sessions by making and quietly sipping tea together before laying out the tasks at hand. I can't say that these activities always led instantly to new and creative ideas. However, I was clear that these breaks and pauses were an important part of our overall creative process. In order to be sure I took this time, I often put these break times onto my calendar.

Today, one of my regular routines occurs before my longest break of the day, when I am getting ready for sleep. When I lie down in bed, I often pay attention to my breathing and gently put my hands on my chest. I then think of a particular issue or problem in my work or my nonbusiness life that I need to think more clearly about. As the idea arises in my mind, I imagine some kind of hint or direction appearing during the night, during my dreams, or perhaps when I'm partly awake during the middle of the night. I have tremendous faith in my unconscious mind.

When I awake in the morning I often sit quietly for a few minutes; sometimes I write in my journal. Very often I'm able to capture insights that have come to me through the benefit of sleep and rest. This morning time of sitting or writing is generally my most creative time of the day. The *New Yorker* article I cite above discusses this: "Jung-Beeman said, 'The problem with the morning, though, is that we're always so rushed. We've got to get the kids ready for school, so we leap out of bed and never give ourselves a chance to think.' [Jung-Beeman] recommends that, if we're stuck on a difficult problem, it's better to set the alarm clock a few minutes early so that we have time to lie in bed and ruminate. We do some of our best thinking when we're still half asleep."

Try these practices for yourself: Every day, schedule a ten-minute break during the afternoon. Walk outside and just pay attention to your walking, to your breath, to whatever is around you. Let go of any agenda, of trying to solve any problem. As thoughts arise in your consciousness, note them, but always return your awareness to walking, breath, body, and environment.

Then, at the end of the day, as you lie down for sleep, put your hands on your chest and take a few deep breaths. Let your breath and your belly soften. Allow a question or issue to float into your awareness. Open yourself to different ways of approaching and understanding the question or issue. Upon waking in the morning, again, take a few gentle breaths and allow the question to surface. Do any new insights come to you? Do you have any new direction about your next steps?

STUDY YOURSELF: FORGET YOURSELF

To study Buddhism is to study yourself. To study yourself is to forget yourself. To forget yourself is to awaken with everyone and everything.

— Eihei Dogen, thirteenth-century founder of Zen in Japan

A turning point in my life came during my freshman year at college when I read *Toward a Psychology of Being* by Abraham Maslow. Maslow devoted much of his life to studying people's happiness and emotions. In particular, he wanted to know why some people experienced better health, well-being, and what he coined self-actualization. These people also had more "peak experiences" — moments of deep emotion and belonging. As a nineteen-year-old growing up in New Jersey, I found this to be an astonishing idea — that certain people could be more developed than others, and that through studying yourself and transforming yourself, you could change and develop emotionally and find a deep sense of peace and belonging. I couldn't imagine anything more important or more worthwhile than this self-study.

This practice of studying yourself requires an attitude of curiosity — just wondering, opening, watching for what happens next without expecting anything. It also requires appreciating just being alive — appreciating this moment, this body, this breath, and seeing the people in our lives in a way that is fresh, open, without assumptions. It also requires a certain level of fearlessness — that is, seeing your fear, your tight spots, and little by little moving toward the fear, toward what is not known. Being afraid and still stepping forward.

How else do you study yourself? When Dogen says study yourself, I think he means more than study: to understand, penetrate, and transform.

Then what does Dogen mean by "forget yourself"? Forgetting yourself means loosening your hold on your beliefs and habits. As we saw in chapter 7, clinging to our familiar and comfortable identity, resisting change — these actions are based in fear and they undermine our efforts and harm our self-worth. Truly believing we have self-worth does not make us narcissistic. Quite the opposite. When we are truly happy about ourselves, we extend our relaxed and generous spirit to others. True self-worth helps us not act from fear. So, forgetting yourself means being fully present and open to whatever situation arises — at least as best you can. It's amazing how doing this can allow us to feel calm and ready to meet whatever life may bring.

When we are truly happy about ourselves, we extend our relaxed and generous spirit to others.

Practice Perspective

As a way to learn how to "forget yourself," try this: Think of a particularly difficult situation you experienced recently — it could be a challenge or problem at work, at home, or in a relationship. In your journal, first describe this situation from the perspective of being a victim. If you had no personal responsibility for the problem, what would you say? Second, describe the same situation as if you had complete responsibility for all aspects of the situation. What would it look like if it was all your fault? Third, describe the same situation as if you were a neutral observer. What would this situation look like if you had stood on the outside and watched it unfold in front of you? How did you feel describing the situation from each perspective? What did you learn about yourself, and about forgetting yourself? Did it lift your spirits? Even better, could you laugh at yourself, even a little?

SLOW DOWN TO MOVE FAST

Speed kills. This is literally true when it comes to driving. The higher the speed, the greater the chances of fatalities. It is also true that working with speed and intensity, without modulating your activity, contributes to a host of physical ailments leading to a variety of health problems and a shortened life.

But often life itself moves fast, and we are challenged to move fast enough to keep up with it. Whether we are a work-all-night CEO or a stay-at-home parent, our days can become filled with the nonstop challenges of business, home, parenting, and relationships: phones ringing, emails flying, reports piling up, meetings and deadlines, children needing to be picked up from school, dinner to make, laundry to do, bills to pay, and so on. When problems arise, we sometimes must make split-second decisions and adjustments.

We are, in fact, not unlike a major league baseball hitter standing at home plate waiting for a ball to be thrown. The pitcher stands just 90 feet away, and we don't know what he'll throw: a curveball, a fastball, a pitch high or low. However, we know the ball can reach speeds of ninety miles per hour, and we'll have less than a second to decide whether and then how to swing.

Our margin for error is razor thin. Consider these numbers:

- A 90 mph fastball can reach home plate in 400 milliseconds — or four-tenths of a second.
- A batter has just a quarter-second to identify the pitch and decide whether to swing and where to swing.

Decision making doesn't get much faster, but surprisingly, some of the most successful baseball players say that as the ball leaves the pitcher's hand, it is as though the world slows down. The batter's experience is that there is plenty of time to decide whether to swing, though the actual time is about a tenth of a second. To achieve this, batters try to feel relaxed, spacious, and at ease, rather than rushed or pressured. Batters need to react almost faster than they can think, and any tension, any distraction, will slow down their reaction time. Of course, baseball pitchers know this and so they vary their pitches in what they hope are unpredictable ways; all they need is to put a split second of doubt in the hitter's mind.

As in baseball, I've noticed that many of the most successful people find ways to slow down their worlds in the midst of what appear to be highly pressured, fast-moving situations. How do they do this? There are three primary practices for slowing down your world: preparation, mindfulness, and focus.

Preparation

When a batter is "on deck" (or next in line to bat), he practices by getting used to the throwing motion and speed of the pitcher. The batter gets accustomed, physically and mentally, to the pitcher's pace. The batter creates a "laboratory" for experimentation. Every time he bats he pays attention, both while on deck and while batting. Though no experience is exactly the same, the patterns are similar.

As Michelangelo famously claimed, his vision when sculpting was to remove the unnecessary marble to expose the statue within. Similarly, our lives are endowed with tremendous unrevealed energy and possibility. Our challenge is to take away the distractions and impediments, allowing us to feel and enter the often invisible or hard-to-find current of our lives. Hitting and sculpting then become a lot easier.

Mindfulness

In the midst of challenging situations, pay attention to your breath and body as a way of grounding and settling yourself. Focus your attention fully on your activity. As distractions arise, note them and let them go. Pay attention to the speed and pace of your activities, and allow your responses to come quickly and appropriately.

Focus

You can do only one thing at a time. Be aware of where you place your attention. If you become distracted, keep returning to your point of focus. Over time, you can increase your ability to stay with one thing, to concentrate and complete tasks. In some situations you may want to experiment with focusing on not focusing. This is a way of keeping your mind open and relaxed while holding an intention to find a solution or perhaps to come to the right question.

TO NAVIGATE TURBULENCE, RELAX

For our family vacations when our children were younger, we often went river rafting. Rafting meant we could be together as a family, interact with the beauty of nature, and meet other people (including our frequently colorful river guides). Plus, it was adventurous, and being on the river meant our family never had to ask that deadliest of questions: "What are we going to do today?" It was always clear — get in the boat and paddle downstream! This was our method for accomplishing more family intimacy with less effort.

We also found that the river is always a great teacher. For example, sometimes your boat goes through a particularly difficult rapid and you find yourself tossed out of the boat and into the water. When this happens, sometimes you get caught in a hole, where the water is churning, or recirculating, back upstream. What do you do? The natural tendency is to vigorously attempt to swim downstream, but in this situation, the water is circulating backward, so you are actually swimming against the current. This is very dangerous; particularly in very cold water, it is quite possible to exhaust yourself fighting the current and be unable to get out of the hole. Unfortunately, people have died this way. However, if you give up swimming and relax, the water pulls you in and for an instant takes you upstream. Usually, this is enough for you to be quickly "spit out" of the hole and sent safely on your way downstream.

Though it's counterintuitive, the most productive and safest action to take in this thrown-in-the-water situation is to relax and let the current take you. At first, the water takes you in the opposite direction from where you want to go, but this is the only way to get out of the rapid and back into the flow of the river. By relaxing, by doing less, you accomplish your goal.

A similar situation came up in a recent coaching meeting I had with a high-ranking engineer of a Fortune 100 company, who described his week as feeling as though he were "swimming upstream." The more pressure he felt, the harder he worked. The harder he worked, the less time he spent with his managers, and with his family. He was unaware that by working harder he was ignoring his important leadership roles — creating a shared vision and then clarifying the vital connections between each team member's work and this shared vision.

For example, in our meeting, he told me that he was scheduled to give an important presentation the next day to his supervisor and team, but he was not at all prepared. The focus of this presentation was to describe the progress his team had made for the first half of the year.

He had become so involved in fighting the daily battles that he had completely lost sight of the larger stream, the more vital priorities of his leadership role and his own career trajectory. For my client, improving the situation required letting go of the incredible tangle of daily issues submerging him, finding his composure in the chaos surrounding him, and getting back into the water's main flow, which is where his immediate and more important work priorities were.

Learning to Swim

Identify the holes in your life. Where are you trying to overcome turbulent busyness through more effort rather than relaxing and letting it go? How might you be struggling toward safety in ways that keep you from reaching the more sustaining current of your life?

Notice where you are fighting the current. What would happen if you relaxed and went with the current? Identify fears that may be holding you back. What do you gain and what do you lose by staying where you are?

EMBRACE PARADOX

A paradox is something that appears to be contradictory, unbelievable, or absurd but may in fact be true. Do less. Accomplish more. These statements present a paradox. Acknowledging, owning, and embracing the paradoxical nature of our lives, the lives of others, and the world can lessen our resistance to change and increase our effectiveness. At its most basic it makes us less tense and more open to happiness.

When I look at my own life and self, I see that I embody a number of paradoxes. Here are a few:

> I am shy and solitary, and I love speaking in front of people.
>
> At work, I am completely myself, and I play a role.
>
> I am firm and decisive, and I am cautious and conservative.
>
> I am a businessman, and I am a Zen priest.
>
> I can concentrate for long periods of time, and I'm easily distracted.
>
> I am confident, and I'm extremely vulnerable.

Each of us contains similar paradoxes. The more we look for them, the more we see paradoxes everywhere — in the world of the heart, in the world of work, and in society. Acknowledging and understanding this basic truth can be freeing. What a relief to not have to make ourselves, others, and life fit neatly into some limited idea or framework! Intuitively we know that all humans are complex and contradictory. Embracing our paradoxes not only provides real insights into ourselves and allows for more self-acceptance but also increases our appreciation of everyone else's surprising quirks and contradictions.

What a relief to not have to make ourselves, others, and life fit neatly into some limited idea or framework!

Sometimes we get caught up trying to resolve internal contradictions, thinking that if we can, we will solve our busyness. Instead, this effort can itself become the cause of our busyness and our scrambled bewilderment. Our complex minds, emotions, and personality traits are simply a rather wonderful fact of human existence. Accepting that can lighten and expand our self-image, making it more fluid. In a strange way it is a more accurate view of life.

Embrace paradox and you increase self-acceptance, tolerance of others, and your own possibilities.

Describe Your Paradoxes

At a recent workshop for a group of engineering managers, I gave everyone the assignment to describe himself or herself as a paradox. Here is what Chade-Meng Tan, a Google engineer whose official title is Jolly Good Fellow, had to say:

> I strive hard to be lazy.
>
> I'm selfishly compassionate.
>
> I desire to not want.
>
> Sometimes, I'm not myself.
>
> Often, I'm not here, where I am.
>
> I actively engage in nonactivity.
>
> I feel spiritual about my earthly desires.
>
> I sometimes fail at failing.
>
> I make careless mistakes carefully.
>
> Sometimes, my mind is full of nothing.
>
> My own arrogance humbles me.
>
> I've become a famous unknown.
>
> I sometimes pity the more fortunate.

Now it is your turn. List the paradoxes that describe yourself. In what ways do you embody contradiction and inconsistency?

Next, explore each of these paradoxes in your journal. Each morning or evening, choose one of your paradoxes and describe it more fully. How does it express itself in your actions and emotions?

If you have trouble coming up with paradoxes, here is a list to get you started. To one degree or another, we all embody these paradoxes. Take one at a time and explore how they apply to you:

> I make precise observations, and I act with abandon.
>
> I like to have clear plans, and I like to forget my plans.

I am predictable, and I am unpredictable.

I love structure and clarity, and I love flexibility.

I like to study myself, and I like to forget about myself.

I am strong, and I am flexible.

I don't take anything personally, and I take everything personally.

I see my work as sacred and mundane.

I am organized and disciplined, and I am creative and innovative.

I am strong and decisive, and I am vulnerable.

I am young, and I am old.

If we can embrace and digest the truth of paradox, it can increase tolerance, respect, and understanding, aid conflict resolution, and act as a bridge for solving all sorts of personal, interpersonal, and global differences and problems.

ALIGNMENT REDUCES BUSYNESS

If we are working harder than ever and still not accomplishing very much, we need to see whether we suffer from a lack of alignment. Alignment sounds jargon-y, but it simply refers to making sure our efforts support our goals. Making sure we are in alignment is key for reducing busyness and increasing effectiveness.

A clear example of this comes from when I worked as a draft horse farmer at Green Gulch Farm over twenty-five years ago. Each spring we would plow the fields in preparation for planting, and the plow was pulled by two horses (during my tenure, Snip and Jerry). I sat on a seat above a large rounded metal blade that dug into the ground. Often one horse would walk faster and pull harder than the other, resulting in the plow's veering off to one side. This made the overall movement of the plow awkward, jerky, and effortful. I would pull back on the horse going ahead and encourage the horse falling behind to go faster. Often they would then overcompensate, and the plow would veer off in the other direction. Then at times both horses would walk together and pull together, nicely aligned. When this happened, not only did the plow move straight ahead but the blade dug more deeply into the ground with much less resistance and effort. With both horses walking in alignment, a field could be plowed in half the time it took when the horses were out of alignment. This was easier both for me and for Snip and Jerry.

INTERNAL ALIGNMENT: While achieving internal alignment in ourselves is much more complex than aligning a pair of horses, the principle is the same. We often swirl with motivations, goals, aspirations, fears, and doubts, all circling around and competing for attention in our head. Our challenge is to get all these desires and emotions in alignment — we must manage our aspirations, visions, goals, doubts, and fears so we keep moving in the same direction. Since we can never be completely free of doubts and fears, this means unearthing and acknowledging our doubts and negative voices and doing what we can to keep them from getting in our way. One way we get out of alignment is by lacking focus and clarity about our direction and our objectives. Another way we get out of alignment is by not recognizing our internal critics and fears; since they are there anyway, they can subtly or not so subtly work against what we want to achieve.

RELATIONSHIP ALIGNMENT: People in relationships are in alignment when both people are working under the same set of assumptions, when they have similar levels of trust and a mutual understanding about where the relationship is going. Conflicts occur, of course, even in the best relationships, but if a couple is in alignment, then these disagreements are typically discussed and resolved without upsetting the course of the plow. When relationships are out of alignment — when there is a different set of assumptions regarding the nature of the relationship, the level of intimacy, and the level of commitment — conflicts are more problematic. Indeed, a couple may avoid addressing or exploring a small conflict in order to avoid discussing the deeper ways they are out of alignment. This lack of understanding is masked by assumptions — usually false ones — about the other person's motivations. Eventually, any relationship needs to be in alignment in order to grow.

ORGANIZATIONAL ALIGNMENT: Organizations are in alignment when each person on the team or in the organization understands the larger mission and how his or her actions are connected to it. Organizations are out of alignment when individuals don't fully understand and embrace the mission, goals, and objectives and don't see how their particular activity influences and contributes to the organization. When this occurs, it's important for the senior management team, and especially the most senior leader, to talk with the employees about the organization's mission and to help everyone feel meaningfully engaged in the company's overall goal. One way to engage people in open discussions is to host off-site retreats and/or half-day "visioning" workshops. In this way, staying in alignment is a continual process.

Bringing Yourself into Alignment

When it comes to bringing alignment to all the voices inside yourself, creating consensus is much more effective than majority rule. Let me explain. One of my coaching clients, Roger, has been leading his team within a technology company for the past two years. He is now at a place where he wants to expand his team and to create additional teams in other parts of the country and the world. He is excited about the idea of expanding, and he feels his current team has the capacity to take on additional projects. At the same time he voices many doubts and fears — "I don't have the management skills to take on more people. What if the projects are not successful? Who am I to be leading teams of people? I'm happy with how things are now and would be crazy to implement change," and so on.

If all his internal voices held a vote, expanding the team might win by a 51 to 49 percent majority. However, this would represent a serious lack of alignment: as one side of Roger worked to expand the team, the other half would fight against this effort. A more effective approach would be for Roger to acknowledge his doubts and fears and get their "buy-in" to go along with the plan: "Fully acknowledging my fears and doubts, I will still work to expand my team."

Achieving this kind of alignment can be difficult on our own. Meditation, mindfulness practice, retreats, and the other practices addressed in this book can all help. Yet this can be deep and difficult work. At the risk of sounding self-serving, this is why working with a skilled coach can be so valuable. To understand our own processes, and to untangle our internal conflicts, it can help to have the guidance of someone who has worked with his or her own issues of alignment and who can support you in your deepening exploration and change.

Try This

Name something that you've been struggling with that you wish to accomplish. It can be something small or a large vision. For example, you might say: "I will exercise at least three times per week," or "I will help my team be more focused and productive," or "I will spend more time with my spouse." Phrase your intention clearly. Write it down, or say it out loud. Now, notice all of the other voices that speak to your intention — voices of excitement, of doubt, of fear, perhaps of terror. Write down or say what each of these voices is saying. Keep writing or speaking until you are sure you have heard and acknowledged all of them. Then go back to your original vision. Speak it out loud. Notice how you feel when you write and speak your intention, as well as when you write and speak from the other voices.

Finally, take all your voices or statements and craft a brief soliloquy. Begin by acknowledging your specific doubts and fears ("Even though I am filled with doubt and fear that . . ."). When these are finished, state what your intention is ("Despite these things, I will exercise at the gym for at least an hour three evenings a week . . ."). Finally, add all the positive reasons why you want to pursue this intention (". . . because I will lower my cholesterol, lose weight, have more energy . . ."). When this is done, read your statement out loud, and in the future, whenever you feel yourself losing your alignment around this issue, you can refer to this statement.

In our more-faster-better world, a life filled with extreme busyness can seem inevitable, unavoidable. Having too much to do becomes such a compelling story that it can be difficult to remember that it is a story we choose to write. The fog of bad habits and distractions can obscure our true desires and undermine our efforts. I hope that, by using the practices in this chapter, you can more often find "the one who is not busy." That is the voice of stillness, of authentic power, of relaxation and calm, of doing less even in the midst of your engaged, exuberant, unpredictable, and sacred life.

EPILOGUE

You are perfect, just as you are (and you can use a little improvement).

— Shunryu Suzuki

A DOCTOR FRIEND I HAVE KNOWN for many years was recently severely injured in a head-on collision with a driver who had a seizure on the Golden Gate Bridge. She broke nearly every bone in her body and was in a coma for several months. It is a miracle that she not only has survived but appears to be in the process of a nearly complete recovery. In her online journal, she writes with a sense of deep knowing and powerful urgency: "We must remember to get on with our lives. Do what is important. If you haven't been married, GET MARRIED. If you need to get divorced, get divorced. Just do what is essential and important. That is what matters."

This book is a collection of tools as well as a manual for doing more of what is important and less of what isn't. Some tools and exercises that I offer are blunt and direct and are intended for deep work. Others are more subtle, intended for more refined change. Please explore and experiment; use them in whatever way that helps you. My hope is that this book will function like an extended coaching session, but even more, I intend it as a warmly personal offer for you to become your own best executive coach.

The truth is, you are both carpenter and saw, for you are responsible for keeping the blade, which is yourself, honed. However, *busyness* not only dulls the blade, resulting in unnecessary and ineffectual effort, but can convince us that we don't even have the time to pull out the grinding stone and keep ourselves sharp. Sometimes the day's furious deadlines make us believe we are so busy that we don't even have a minute — much less ten or twenty — to stop, pause, and reflect. We convince ourselves that we can't do the very things that we most want, or the things that would make all our efforts easier and more effective. In short, we become accustomed to using a dull saw, and we may stop even noticing how much extra effort we are exerting for such diminishing returns.

Unlike a carpenter, we don't need to do anything extra to return to our original state of sharpness and unbridled full functioning. We only need to do less of what gets in the way. As Shunryu Suzuki says, "You are perfect just as you are." And, as he adds somewhat cryptically, "You can use a little improvement." When I first read that quote thirty years ago, I found it hard to comprehend. Yes, it was a paradox, but it seemed rather puzzling and not very helpful. Now that I have had many years to ponder it, I believe it is one of the kindest and most freeing pieces of wisdom to live by.

What is interesting is that we usually become overbusy for

laudable reasons — we are pursuing our dreams, being responsible citizens, assisting our family members or colleagues, and seeking happiness and real freedom. Having a lot to do is not innately a bad thing. Most of us love being active. I do. But this becomes over-the-top busyness when it makes us feel depleted rather than complete, when we run down the path toward freedom and real accomplishment but find them getting farther away.

THE POWER OF SABBATH

When my two children were in elementary school, a weekly day of doing less was an important part of our family ritual. We borrowed some ideas from the Jewish Sabbath as well as Buddhist Day of Mindfulness practices. At the heart of our day we had three simple rules that we applied from sundown on Friday until sundown on Saturday evening:

Rule #1: There was no spending money.

Rule #2: There was no watching television.

Rule #3: We did something together as a family.

These three guidelines produced significant results in the quality of those twenty-four hours. What a relief to not buy anything, not have the television on, and spend time simply enjoying each other's presence. My wife and I talked more with our two children; we read books, told stories, played games, went for walks, and shared meals. The biggest benefit of this structured break was that, for a day, the pace of our lives slowed down and our family connections increased.

One of my favorite parts of this ritual was the formal ending. We observed the Jewish tradition of looking for the first three stars to become visible on Saturday evening, signaling that Sabbath was over. It was fun and exciting for the four of us to stand on our deck together, seeing who could find the three stars as the sun faded and nighttime slowly emerged. Of course, since we live in Marin County, dense fog sometimes forced us to use our imaginations.

Instituting rest and simplicity is not a magic wand for perfection. There were occasional disagreements, grumpiness, and boredom. But our imperfections often emerge as the most endearing parts of ourselves, and those "Sabbath" days stand out as important building blocks, and are great memories, for our still-growing family.

YOU ARE PERFECT THE WAY YOU ARE

See if you can fully own the notion that "You are perfect, just as you are." Really let it seep into your mind and body, into your bones. This is a fundamental understanding of the Less Manifesto. We are born with all the wisdom, playfulness, and imagination we need; we just sometimes need help and reminders to return to our senses and get out of our own way. It is the firm knowledge that nothing extra is required. You have everything you need; just let go of whatever distractions, fears, and busyness might be hampering you. It's that simple. Allow yourself to think and feel and live that way. Acting from this place results in greater composure, and when we act with composure, we are more effective.

> We are born with all the wisdom, playfulness, and imagination we need; we just sometimes need help and reminders to return to our senses and get out of our own way.

At the same time, we must embrace the paradox that, despite being perfect, we can all "use a little improvement." Needing "improvement" does not make us less perfect, just the way we are. Instead, this idea simply recognizes that nothing is stagnant;

everything is changing. There is always the possibility for developing more awareness, in this moment. We can almost always develop ways to work better and increase our effectiveness; we can always find more ways to benefit others and improve our lives and our world. That is why we are on this planet. Of course, change brings the possibility of pain, of failure, and of new problems to solve. May you meet them, too, with less effort, more composure, more effectiveness, and greater joy.

ACKNOWLEDGMENTS

I HOPE TO TAKE A MINIMALIST APPROACH to saying thanks: saying less, and yet expressing the deep gratitude I feel for the generous help I received in writing this book. Using fewer words with greater impact — not so easy! I am indebted to so many people who have helped develop and transmit the ideas, practices, and challenges that inform this book.

First, a thank-you to Jennifer Futernick, a friend and editor whom I met over twenty years ago. When I think back to our first meeting about this book, I remember the disorganized, illogical draft I placed on her kitchen table. She politely declined and explained that she was not working on any more books. Then something changed. I suspect she could not resist the challenge. Her "no" was soon followed by a full-hearted "yes." I am so appreciative of the many drafts back and forth, the spirited debates, and her close attention to the power of each word. She has influenced and shaped this book, and me, immensely, for the better.

Many thanks to the skilled and compassionate editors and allies at New World Library. I am particularly thankful to Jason Gardner, senior editor, for having faith in the potential of this book and giving wise counsel as I struggled to mesh ancient traditions with pressing contemporary issues. Jeff Campbell offered excellent insight and writing skill with kindness, as copyeditor, making this a better book. Thank you, Munro Magruder for getting the book out into the world with much grace and perseverance.

I'm grateful for my many teachers, mentors, and friends who inspired the book's ideas and practices, especially Norman Fischer, Michael Wenger, Lewis Richmond, Harry Roberts, Chade-Meng Tan, Jackie McGrath, and Sheri Syler Adams.

Much appreciation and gratitude to Robert Gass, teacher, mentor, and friend. Many ideas and practices here were inspired by the deep work of the Art of Leadership workshops.

Thanks for the help and support of the San Francisco Zen Center, where I grew up and which I continue to call my spiritual home.

Thanks to the leadership and members of Social Venture Network — friends and colleagues who bring conscience, clarity, and a higher purpose to the world of work.

Thank you Chris Fortin, Peter Walsh, Liza Braude-Blidden, Serena Hazard, Patricia Ryan Madson, and Eta Morris for your honest feedback as well as your tremendous personal support.

And thank you to my wife, Lee, for being a wise and compassionate partner, friend, and editor; for asking the difficult questions and always raising the bar — about this book, and about our lives.

SOURCES AND
RECOMMENDED READING

Allen, David. *Getting Things Done*. New York: Penguin, 2002.

Bargh, John A., and Tanya L. Chartrand. "The Unbearable Automaticity of Being." *American Psychologist*, July 1999.

Brooks, David. "The Neural Buddhists." *The New York Times*, May 13, 2008.

Bruch, Heike, and Sumantra Ghoshal. "Beware the Busy Manager." *Harvard Business Review*, February 2002.

Carr, Nicholas. "Is Google Making Us Stupid?" *The Atlantic*, July/August 2008.

Chödrön, Pema. *Practicing Peace in Times of War*. Boston: Shambhala, 2008.

Coburn, David. "Baseball Physics: Anatomy of a Home Run." *Popular Mechanics*, June 2007.

Cohen, Darlene. *The One Who Is Not Busy*. Layton, UT: Gibbs Smith, 2004.

Covey, Stephen. *First Things First*. New York: Free Press, 1994.

Fischer, Norman. *Sailing Home*. New York: Free Press, 2008.

Goleman, Daniel. *Working with Emotional Intelligence*. New York: Bantam, 2000.

Imai, Masaaki. *Gemba Kaizen*. New York: McGraw-Hill, 1997.

Kabat-Zinn, Jon. *Full Catastrophe Living*. New York: Bantam, 1990.

Katagiri, Dainin. *Each Moment Is the Universe*. Boston:
   Shambhala, 2007.

Lehrer, Jonah. "The Eureka Hunt." *The New Yorker*,
   July 28, 2008.

Levy, David. "No Time to Think." *Ethics and Information
   Technology*, December 2007.

Lohr, Jim, and Tony Schwartz. "The Making of a Corporate
   Athlete." *Harvard Business Review*, January 2001.

Martin, Roger, and Hilary Austen. "The Art of Integrative
   Thinking." *Rotman Management*, Fall 1999.

Maslow, Abraham. *Toward a Psychology of Being*. New York:
   Wiley, 1961.

Muller, Wayne. *Sabbath*. New York: Bantam, 1999.

Pally, Regina. "The Predicting Brain: Unconscious Repetition,
   Conscious Reflection and Therapeutic Change." *The
   International Journal of Psychoanalysis*, September 2006.

Ray, Michael, and Rochelle Myers. *Creativity in Business*. New
   York: Doubleday/Main Street Books, 1986.

Rosenthal, Robert, and Lenore Jacobson. *The Pygmalion Effect*.
   Crown House Publishing, 2003.

Shoemaker, Fred. *Extraordinary Golf*. New York: Perigee Trade,
   1976.

Siegel, Daniel J. *The Mindful Brain*. New York: W. W. Norton,
   2007.

Suzuki, Shunryu. *Not Always So*. New York: HarperCollins,
   2002.

Taylor, Jill Bolte. *My Stroke of Insight*. New York: Viking, 2008.

INDEX

A

accomplishment, 7
    defining, 15
    doing less and, 13–14, 15–16,
        134–35, 144–46
    envisioning, 99–100
    fluidity and, 44–45
    meaning of, 111–12
    sense of, 15
    See also effectiveness
alignment, 149–53
Allen, David, 96
anchoring, 79–80
anger, 76–80
annoyance, 60
answers, searching for, 61–62
anxiety, 38, 82
    See also fear(s)
Archimedes, 136, 138
asking
    for benefit of experience, 86–87
    for feedback, 70, 71, 72–73
    help offers, 87–88
    knowledge through, 84
    positive results from, 86–87
    request-making, 85–86
aspirations, clarifying, 96
assumptions
    asking for help and, 83–87

conflict based on, 66–68
defined, 69
    in everyday life, 65
    false, 65–68, 81–82
    feedback and, 70–72
    identifying, 68–70, 82–83
    as Less Manifesto category, 30,
        34
    self-awareness and, 80–81
    speaking up about, 81–83
    testing / verifying, 68
    triggers and, 76–78
Atlantic, The, 89–90
attitudes
    nonjudgmental, 131
    open-ended, 118–19
    outcomes influenced by, 117–18
    self-defeating, 116–19
avoidance, 4, 120–21

B

Bargh, John A., 116
Beatles, The, 68
beliefs. See attitudes
benchmarks, 121–22, 130
Berry, Wendell, 86
"Beware the Busy Manager" (Bruch
    and Ghoshal), 92
bodywork, 135

breaks
  assumptions decharged
    through, 78–80
  creative breakthroughs and,
    136–40
  doing less through, 14
  mini-breaks, as routine, 102–4
  stress breaks, 104, 105
breathing, 44, 50–51, 91
  See also meditation
Brooks, David, 13
Bruch, Heike, 92
Brush Dance, 17–18, 66–67, 74,
  81–82, 128
Buddhism
  change in, 113
  Day of Mindfulness in, 157
  five primary fears in, 38
  generosity in, 62
  monkey mind in, 57–58
  present moment in, 41–42, 140
  See also Zen Buddhism
business plans, 121
busy, being, 3–4, 133–34
busyness
  addiction to, 8
  alignment and, 149–53
  being busy vs., 4, 133–34
  communications technology
    and, 9–10
  culture of, 8–9
  defined, 4
  dulling effect of, 156
  fear and, 64
  as Less Manifesto category, 30,
    35–36
  mental, quieting, 5–6, 8
  paradox and, 146–49
  reasons for, 156–57
  relaxing and, 144–46
  self-study and, 140–42
  signs of, 4
  slowing down and, 142–44

  unnecessary activity and,
    135–36, 155–56
  unsustainability of, 8–9

C

Carr, Nicholas, 89–90
cell phones, 9–10
center, accessing, 47, 58
"CEO disease," 74
change
  attitudes and, 116–19, 132
  creativity and, 126–28, 132
  emotional, 120
  integrative thinking and,
    123–26, 132
  perfection as one is and, 158–59
  precise observations and, 121–23
  resistance to, 113–16, 128
  small, Kaizen and, 129–32
  systems creation and, 122–23
Chartrand, Tanya L., 116
Chödrön, Pema, 79
choices, 111–12, 123–26
commercialism, 157
Committee on Recent Economic
  Changes, 111
communications technology, 9–10,
  89–90, 138
composure
  distractions and, 91–92
  doing less and, 7
  effectiveness and, 80, 112
  as generosity, 62
  visual images for, 20–21
computers, 9–10
concentration, impact of communications technology on, 89–90
conflict
  alignment and, 150–51
  false assumptions and, 66–68
conscious wandering, 137–38
Conservatree Paper, 17

conversation, 52, 81
creativity
    breaks essential for, 136–40
    inspiring, 126–28, 132
current events, busyness and, 4–5

D

Dalai Lama, 105
daydreaming, 98
decision-making, 142–43
deep power, accessing, 6–7
desires, 111–12, 114
details, paying attention to, 127–28
difficulties, avoidance of, 4
digital technology, 9–10
dipping, 75–76
distractedness, 90–91
distractions
    choice-making and, 111–12
    from communications technol-
      ogy, 89–90
    defined, 90
    distractedness vs., 90–91
    envisioning success and,
      99–100
    as Less Manifesto category, 30,
      34–35
    managing, 92–94
    meetings, 100–101
    need for, 137–38
    reduction strategies, 94–99
    routines and, 105
    by searching for answers,
      61–62
    types of, 90–91
distractions quotient, 102
Dogen, Eihei, 41–42, 140, 141
doing less
    and accomplishing more, 13–14,
      15–16, 134–35, 144–46
    benefits of, 23–24
    courage required for, 25

defined, 7–8
difficulty of, 33
doing nothing vs., 11
five ways of, 14
guiding principle of, 13–14
hunger for, 10–12
as paradox, 146–49
at work, 30–34

E

effectiveness
    busyness vs., 10
    composure within realm of,
      20–21, 91–92
    effortlessness combined with,
      134–35
    feedback and, 70
    managerial, 92–94, 100–102,
      123–24, 151
    resistance and, 115–16
    slowing down as means to, 36
    visual images of, 20–21
    See also accomplishment
effort, effortlessness integrated with,
    14, 134–35
Einstein, Albert, 44
email, 9, 93, 96–97
emotions
    changing, 120
    loss of control, 4
    painful, 46
energy, 7, 40
"eureka" moments, 136–37
exercise, 107
exhales, counting, 50–51
expectations, letting go of, 59
Extraordinary Golf (Shoemaker), 134

F

failure, 18–19
family retreats, 57

fear(s)
  acknowledgment/awareness
    of, 38–39, 63–64
  alignment and, 150
  as ally, 37
  busyness as escape from, 64
  elimination of, 63
  fluidity and, 44–45
  generosity as antidote to, 31,
    60–62
  as hindrance, 37–38
  impermanence and, 95
  as Less Manifesto category, 30, 34
  listing/acting upon, 62–63
  paying attention to, 31
  primary, in Buddhism, 38
  reducing, through meditation,
    46–52
  reducing, through retreats,
    52–60
  relaxing and, 146
  self-study and, 141
  time and, 39–44
feedback
  asking for, 70, 71, 72–73
  assumptions and, 70–72
  effectiveness through, 70
  listening to, 73–76
  in practice, 75–76
festering, 81–83
Fidelity Investments, 129–30
"Finding the One Who Is Not
  Busy," 35
flexible mind, 108–9
fluidity, 44–46, 50–51, 108–9
focus
  alignment and, 150
  doing less and, 7
  meditation for, 23
  overfocus, 138
  reducing distractions for, 91,
    95–99
  slowing down through, 144
  visual images for, 20–21

forgetting oneself, 41, 140–42
Franklin, Benjamin, 40

G

Gandhi, Mohandas, 53
Gates, Bill, 52–53
Gemba Kaizen (Imai), 129
generosity, 31, 60–62
Getting Things Done (Allen), 96
Ghoshal, Sumantra, 92
Gladwell, Malcolm, 116
global issues, busyness and, 4–5
goals, long-term vs. short-term, 15
Goleman, Daniel, 120
gratitude, 60–62, 74
Green Gulch Farm (Muir Beach,
  CA), 5, 44–45, 66, 149–50

H

habits
  diffusing, 96–98
  paying attention to, 58
  self-defeating, five categories
    of, 29–30 (see also assump-
    tions; busyness; distractions;
    fear(s); resistance)
  See also routines
Hafiz (poet), 105
happiness, 70, 105–6
Harvard Business Review, 92, 93, 103
heart, fierce and tender, 7
help
  asking for, 83–87
  offers of, 87–88
Hoover, Herbert, 111
How Successful Leaders Think
  (Martin), 123–24

I

Imai, Masaaki, 129
immutability, 44

impatience, 46, 60
impermanence, 45, 95–96, 113–14
    See also change
integrative thinking, 123–26, 132
Internet, 9–10, 89–90, 138
interruptions, 89
    See also distractions
"Is Google Making Us Stupid?"
    (Carr), 89–90

J

Jackson, Maggie, 89
Jacobson, Lenore, 118
James, William, 89
Johnson, Edward C., III, 129
journal writing, 52, 81, 107
Judaism, Sabbath in, 157–58
Jung-Beeman, Mark, 137, 139

K

Kaizen, 129–32
kindness, 23–24, 112
knowledge, 84
Krishnamurti, J., 37

L

language, 84
Lesser, Marc, background of, 16–18
    See also Brush Dance; Green
        Gulch Farm; San Francisco
        Zen Center; Tassajara Zen
        Mountain Center; ZBA
        Associates
Less Manifesto, 13
    five core practices of, 29–30,
        34–36 (*see also* assumptions;
        busyness; distractions;
        fear(s); resistance)
    perfection as one is and, 158–59
Levy, David, 110–11
listening, 70, 73–76, 79
Lohr, Jim, 103

looping, 75–76
love, 23–24, 112

M

"Making of a Corporate Athlete,
    The" (Lohr and Schwartz), 103
management retreats, 56
managers, effective, 92–94, 100–102,
    123–24, 151
Martin, Roger, 123–24
Maslow, Abraham, 140
measurements, 121–22, 130
meditation, 10
    alignment through, 152
    author's experience with,
        16–18, 46–47
    basic instructions for, 31
    benefits of, 23
    "counting your exhales," 50–51
    as daily routine, 105, 106
    defined, 46
    as distraction, 91
    doing less through, 14
    fear reduced through, 46–52
    fluidity and, 45–46, 50–51
    journal writing as, 52
    practice, 47, 48–50, 98–99
    questions to ask yourself dur-
        ing, 50
    resistance to, 47–48
    self-awareness through, 69
    sitting, 11
    tradition of, 17
    walking, 14
    at workplace, 21–23, 30–34
    See also mindfulness; mindful-
        ness practice
meetings, 93, 100–101, 117
Michelangelo, 143
mind
    flexible, 108–9
    management of, 40
    ordinary, 88

Mindful Brain, The (Siegel), 92
mindfulness
    day set aside for, 57, 157–58
    quieting busyness through,
        5–6
    routine for, 105, 138–39
    slowing down through, 144
    use of term, 51
    visual images for, 20–21
mindfulness practice
    absolute time achieved
        through, 45
    alignment through, 152
    as distraction, 91
    doing less through, 14
    fear reduced through, 51–52
    as "sabbath," 157–58
mini-breaks, 102–4
monkey mind, 57–58
multitasking, 8, 10, 91, 94
mundanity, sacred blended with, 59
My Stroke of Insight (Taylor), 43

N

New Yorker, 137, 139
New York University, 17
Nhat Hanh, Thich, 73
"no festering" rule, 81–83

O

observations, precise, 120–23
ordinary mind, 88
organizations, alignment in, 151
Ovid, 117–18

P

pace, changing, 57
Pally, Regina, 65
paradox, embracing, 146–49, 156,
    158–59
patience, 24, 85–86

pausing, 79
peak experiences, 140
Peer, Shahar, 102–3
perfection, as one is, 155, 156, 158–59
personal retreats, 56
perspective
    finding new, 57
    practicing, 141–42
phone calls, 93, 96, 97, 138
Poincaré, Jules-Henri, 126–27
Practicing Peace in a Time of War
    (Chödrön), 79
predictions, 65
    See also assumptions
preparation, 143–44
present moment, focus on, 14, 41–43,
    94–95
pretense, 4
priming, 116, 132
prioritizing, 92–94
problems, engaging, 23
productivity management, 40
purpose management, 40
Pygmalion Effect, 118
Pygmalion in the Classroom (Rosen-
    thal and Jacobson), 118

R

Ray, Michael, 127–28
reflection, 14
relationships, alignment in, 150–51
relaxing, 144–46
requests, making, 85–86
resistance
    avoidance as, 120–21
    to change, 113–16, 128
    as Less Manifesto category, 30, 35
    to meditation, 47–48
    precise observations and, 120–23
    reducing, through Kaizen,
        129–32
    self-defeating beliefs and, 116–19
    See also change

rest, 14, 157–58
results, 7, 130
retreats, 14
    alignment through, 152
    author's experience with, 53–55
    as distractions, 91
    fear reduced through, 52–60
    finding, 56
    fluidity attained through, 45
    returning to life following,
        59–60
    tips for, 57–60
    types of, 56–57
Rilke, Rainer Maria, 113
Roberts, Harry, 5–6, 7, 44–45
Rosenthal, Robert, 118
routines
    creativity and, 139
    exercise, 107
    flexibility through, 108–9
    journal writing, 107
    meditation, 105, 106
    as natural, 108
    positive, 105–7, 139–40
    re-creating, 109–10
    as secret of happiness, 105–6
Rutgers University, 5, 16, 17

S

"sabbaths," 57, 157–58
sacred, mundanity blended with, 59
Saint Exupéry, Antoine de, 3, 11
San Francisco Zen Center, 5, 16–17, 46
    See also Green Gulch Farm
Schwartz, Tony, 103
Search Inside Yourself, 131–32
self-awareness, 19, 69–70, 72,
    80–81
self-centeredness, 61
self-doubt, 4, 77
self-judgmentalism, 127
self-study, 41–42, 140–42

self-worth, 141
Shoemaker, Fred, 134
Siegel, Daniel J., 46, 92
sleep, 137, 139–40
slowing down, 142–44
solidness, 44
song
    finding, 5, 6–7
    singing, 5, 7–8
staff retreats, 56
stress, 21
    chronic, 103
    as motivator, 103
    "no festering" rule and, 81–83
    reducing, 93, 98–99, 135
    as sign of busyness, 4
stress breaks, 104, 105
success. See accomplishment
sustainability, 8–9, 91–92
Suzuki, Shunryu, 23, 46, 155, 156
systemic thinking, 130
systems, creating, 122–23

T

talking, 52, 70, 81
Tanahashi, Kazuaki, 60
tasks, three most important, 5
Tassajara Zen Mountain Center, 17,
    109
Taylor, Jill Bolte, 43
television, 138, 157
text-messaging, 9
thinking/thoughts
    clarifying, 52
    integrative, 123–26, 132
    stressful, 21
    systemic, 130
    time for, 93, 97–98
Thoreau, Henry David, 133
time
    borrowed, savoring, 98
    fear and, 34, 39–41

time (*continued*)
　　management of, 39–41
　　obsession with, 39
　　playing with, 43–44
　　for reflection, 93, 97–98
　　relative vs. absolute, 41–43, 45
　　squandering of, 92
timelines, 121–22
Time magazine, 53
time-management techniques, 39–40
"time out," 10
Toward a Psychology of Being
　　(Maslow), 140
triggers, 76–80
trust, 80, 127

U

Unbearable Automaticity of Being,
　　The (Bargh and Chartrand), 116
unhappiness, busyness as excuse for,
　　4
unnecessary activity, reducing
　　distraction management and,
　　　92–93
　　as doing less, 7, 14, 155–56
　　effectiveness improved
　　　through, 135–36
　　Kaizen as means of, 129

V

vision, 15
voices, inner
　　accessing, 19, 46
　　alignment of, 150, 151–52
　　external voices vs., 91
　　judging, 127
vulnerability, 32, 84

W

walking, 139
Wall Street Journal, 53
Web, the, 9–10
weekly "sabbaths," 57
William of Ockham, 29
work, 7
　　doing less at, 30–34
　　"from the inside out," 93–94
　　mini-breaks during, 102–4
　　prioritizing, 92–94
　　as spiritual practice, 17
　　24/7 connection with, 9–10, 91
Working with Emotional Intelligence
　　(Goleman), 120
workplace
　　distractions at, 96–97
　　envisioning success at, 99–100
　　fear at, 44
　　feedback needed at, 70–72
　　goal-setting at, 15
　　meditation at, 21–23, 30–34

Z

ZBA Associates, 18, 124
Z.B.A.: Zen of Business Administra-
　　tion (Lesser), 18
Zen Buddhism, 7
　　author's experience with, 16–18
　　impermanence in, 95
　　ordinary mind in, 88
　　retreats in, 53–55
　　ritual/form as used in, 108–9
　　teaching stories in, 35
　　See also Buddhism
Zen Mind, Beginner's Mind (Suzuki),
　　46

ABOUT THE AUTHOR

MARC LESSER IS THE FOUNDER AND CEO of ZBA Associates, a management consulting, coaching, and training company. For more than twenty years Marc has been integrating mindfulness and awareness practices with business, strategy, and leadership practices to help corporations, organizations, and individuals achieve greater impact and results.

Prior to founding ZBA, Marc was the founder and CEO of Brush Dance, an innovative publisher of greeting cards, calendars, and journals with distribution throughout the U.S. and the world.

Marc has been practicing and studying Zen for more than thirty years and is a Zen teacher in the lineage of Suzuki Roshi, author of *Zen Mind, Beginner's Mind*. Marc was a resident of the San Francisco Zen Center for ten years and, in 1983, served as director of Tassajara Zen Mountain Center, the first Zen monastery in the West.

Marc is the author of *Z.B.A. Zen of Business Administration: How Zen Practice Can Transform Your Work and Your Life*. He has an MBA from New York University's Stern School of Business and a BA degree in psychology from Rutgers University. He lives with his family in Mill Valley, California.

To learn more about ZBA's services, Accomplishing More By Doing Less workshops, and Warmhearted Leadership workshops, visit www.zbaassociates.com or www.accomplishingmorebydoing less.com.